DATE DUE

DEC 1 4 2016	

BRODART, CO.　　　　　　　　　Cat. No. 23-221

The Declaration of Independence: A Study in the History of Political Ideas

Carl Lotus Becker

BIBLIOBAZAAR

THE DECLARATION OF INDEPENDENCE

A STUDY IN THE HISTORY OF POLITICAL IDEAS

BY

CARL BECKER

PROFESSOR OF HISTORY IN CORNELL UNIVERSITY

NEW YORK

HARCOURT, BRACE AND COMPANY

But what is nature? Why is custom not natural? I greatly fear that this nature is itself only a first custom, as custom is a second nature.

PASCAL, *Pensées* (Havet ed., 1897), I, 42.

We need not feel the truth that law is but usurpation; it was introduced without reason, it has become reasonable; it is necessary to cause it to be regarded as authentic, eternal, and to conceal the beginning of it if we do not wish it to come soon to an end.

Ibid., I, 39.

As to the late Civil Wars, 'tis pretty well known, what Notions of Government went current in those Days. When Monarchy was to be subverted, we know what was necessary to justify the Fact; and then, because it was convenient for the purpose, it was undoubtedly true in the Nature of Things, that Government had its Original from the People, and the Prince was only their Trustee. . . . This was the Doctrine that was commonly received, and the only Doctrine that relish'd in those times. But afterwards, when Monarchy took its place again, . . . another Notion of Government came into Fashion. Then Government had its Original entirely from God, and the Prince was accountable to none but Him. . . . And now, upon another turn of things, when people have a liberty to speak out, a new Set of Notions is advanced; now Passive Obedience is all a mistake, and instead of being a duty to suffer Oppression, 'tis a Glorious Act to resist it: and instead of leaving Injuries to be redress'd by God, we have a natural right to relieve ourselves.

TH. BURNETT, *An Essay upon Government*, p. 10.

The constitution of 1795, like all of its predecessors, is made for *Man*. . . . I have seen, in my time, Frenchmen, Italians, Russians, etc.; I even know, thanks to Montesquieu, that one may be a Persian: but as for *Man*, I declare I never met him in my life; if he exists, it is without my knowledge.

DE MAISTRE, *Oeuvres* (ed. 1875), I, 68.

▼

ACKNOWLEDGMENT

To my colleagues, Professor Charles H. Hull and Professor Wallace Notestein, to Mr. Worthington C. Ford, and to Mr. John C. Fitzpatrick, the author is indebted for helpful suggestions in connection with this essay.

The present volume was in plate proofs before I saw Mr. Fitzpatrick's interesting article on The Declaration of Independence in the Daughters of the American Revolution Magazine *for July, 1922. That article should be read in connection with chapter IV of the present work.*

CONTENTS

THE DECLARATION OF INDEPENDENCE

CHAPTER I

THE DECLARATION OF INDEPENDENCE

IT is often forgotten that the document which we know as the Declaration of Independence is not the official act by which the Continental Congress voted in favor of separation from Great Britain. June 7, 1776, Richard Henry Lee, on behalf of the Virginia delegation, submitted to the Continental Congress three resolutions, of which the first declared that "these United Colonies are, and of right ought to be, free and independent States, that they are absolved from all allegiance to the British Crown, and that all political connection between them and the State of Great Britain is, and ought to be, totally dissolved." [1] This resolution, which may conveniently be called the Resolution of Independence, was finally voted by the Continental Congress on the 2 of July, 1776.[2] Strictly speaking, this was the official declaration of independence; and if we were a nation of antiquaries we should no doubt find an incongruity in celebrating the anniversary of our independence on the 4 of July.

[1] *Journals of Congress* (Ford ed.), V, 424. [2] *Ibid.*, 507.

3

Meanwhile, on the 10 of June, three days after Richard Henry Lee introduced the Resolution of Independence, it was voted to appoint a committee to "prepare a declaration to the effect of the said first resolution." The committee, appointed on the following day, consisted of Thomas Jefferson, John Adams, Benjamin Franklin, Roger Sherman, and Robert R. Livingston.[1] On the 28 of June, the committee reported to Congress the draft of a declaration which, with modifications, was finally agreed to by Congress on the 4 of July.[2] This is the document which is popularly known as the Declaration of Independence.

This title is not, strictly speaking, the official title of the document in question. The document never knew itself, in any of its various forms, by that name. Jefferson, in making the first draft, gave it the following title: *A Declaration by the Representatives of the United States of America, in General Congress assembled.* This title was retained in all the copies of the Declaration, except the engrossed parchment copy. On the 19 of July, 1776, Congress voted that the Declaration be engrossed on parchment, "with the title and stile of *The unanimous Declaration of the thirteen united States of America.*" It is true, the Declaration, in the form adopted by

---

[1] *Ibid.*, 428–429, 431.   [2] *Ibid.*, 491, 510.

Congress, incorporates in its final paragraph the resolution of July 2; and so the Declaration may be said to be a declaration of independence, inasmuch as in it Congress once more declared what it had already declared two days before. Nevertheless, the primary purpose of the Declaration was not to declare independence, but to proclaim to the world the reasons for declaring independence. It was intended as a formal justification of an act already accomplished.

The purpose of the Declaration is set forth in the first paragraph — a striking sentence, in which simplicity of statement is somehow combined with an urbane solemnity of manner in such a way as to give that felicitous, haunting cadence which is the peculiar quality of Jefferson's best writing.

When in the course of human events, it becomes necessary for one people to dissolve the political bands, which have connected them with another, and to assume, among the powers of the earth, the separate and equal station, to which the laws of nature and of nature's God entitle them a decent respect to the Opinions of mankind requires that they should declare the causes which impel them to the separation.[1]

[1] There are three texts of the Declaration which may be called official. One is the text in what is called the 'rough' Journal; a second

The ostensible purpose of the Declaration was, therefore, to lay before the world the causes which impelled the colonies to separate from Great Britain. We do in fact find, in the Declaration, a list or catalogue of acts, attributed to the king of Great Britain, and alleged to have been done by him with the deliberate purpose of establishing over the colonies "an absolute tyranny." These "causes" which the Declaration sets forth are not quite the same as those which a careful student of history, seeking the antecedents of the Revolution, would set forth. The reason is that the framers of the Declaration were not writing history, but making it. They were seeking to convince the world that they were justified in doing what they had done; and so their statement of "causes" is not the bare record of what the king had done, but rather a presentation of his acts in general terms, and in the form of an indictment intended

---

is the text in the 'corrected' Journal; a third is the text on parchment, the one which was signed by the members of Congress. The most authoritative text, one would suppose, should be that in the corrected Journal. Apart from spelling, punctuation, and capitalization, this text is the same as that in the rough Journal except in two instances in each of which a single word is omitted from the text in the corrected Journal which appears in the rough Journal. That these omissions were not intentional seems clear from the fact that they were not made in the final parchment copy. Cf. Hazelton, *The Declaration of Independence*, 170, 306, 321, 325. The texts in the rough Journal and on parchment are given below, pp. 174, 185. The text given in this chapter is that of the corrected Journal.

to clear the colonists of all responsibility and to throw all the blame on the king. From whatever causes, the colonists were in rebellion against established and long recognized political authority. The Declaration was not primarily concerned with the causes of this rebellion; its primary purpose was to present those causes in such a way as to furnish a moral and legal justification for that rebellion. The Declaration was essentially an attempt to prove that rebellion was not the proper word for what they were doing.

Rebellion against established authority is always a serious matter. In that day kings were commonly claiming to rule by divine right, and according to this notion there could be no 'right' of rebellion. The framers of the Declaration knew very well that however long their list of grievances against the king of Great Britain might be, and however oppressive they might make out his acts to have been, something more would be required to prove to the world that in separating from Great Britain they were not really engaged in rebellion against a rightful authority. What they needed, in addition to many specific grievances against their particular king, was a fundamental presupposition against kings in general. What they needed was a theory of government that provided a place for rebellion, that made it respectable, and even meritorious under certain circumstances.

Before enumerating the specific grievances against the king of Great Britain, Jefferson therefore proceeded to formulate a general political philosophy — a philosophy upon which the case of the colonies could solidly rest. This philosophy, which affirms the right of a people to establish and to overturn its own government, is formulated in the first part of the second paragraph of the Declaration.

We hold these truths to be self-evident, That all men are created equal, that they are endowed by their creator with certain unalienable rights; that among these are life, liberty & the pursuit of happiness; that to secure these rights governments are instituted among men, deriving their just powers from the consent of the governed; that whenever any form of government becomes destructive of these ends, it is the right of the people to alter or to abolish it, and to institute new government, laying its foundation on such principles and organizing its powers in such form, as to them shall seem most likely to effect their safety and happiness.

This is a frank assertion of the right of revolution, whenever "the people" are convinced that the existing government has become destructive of the ends for which all government is instituted among men. Many difficulties lie concealed in the words "the people"; but it is sufficient to note in passing that a large part of the people in the colonies, not being convinced that the British government had as yet become destructive of their liberties, or for some other reason, were either indifferently or strongly opposed to separation. Yet the leaders of the Revolution, being now committed to independence, found it politically expedient to act on the assumption that the opposition was negligible. Very naturally, therefore, Jefferson endeavored to make it appear that the people of the colonies were thoroughly united in wishing to 'institute new government' in place of the government of the king.

Accordingly, having affirmed the right of revolution under certain conditions, the Declaration goes on to state that as a matter of fact these conditions prevail in the colonies, and that 'the people' have submitted to them as long as it is humanly possible to do.

Prudence, indeed, will dictate, that governments long established should not be changed for light and transient causes; and accordingly all experience hath shewn that mankind are more disposed to suffer, while evils are sufferable than to right themselves by abolishing the forms, to which they are accustomed. But when a long train of abuses & usurpations pursuing invariably the same object evinces a design to reduce them under absolute despotism, it is their right, it is their duty to throw off such government and to provide new guards for their future security. — Such has been the patient sufferance of these colonies, and such is now the necessity, which constrains them to alter their former systems of government. The history of the present king of great Britain is a history of repeated injuries and usurpations, all having in direct object the establishment of an absolute tyranny over these states. To prove this let facts be submitted to a candid world.

So at last we come to the 'facts,' the list or catalogue of oppressive measures, the 'repeated injuries and usurpations' of the king of Great Britain.

He has refused his assent to laws the most wholesome and necessary for the public good.

He has forbidden his governors to pass laws of immediate and pressing importance, unless suspended in their operation until his assent should be obtained, and when so suspended, he has utterly neglected to attend to them.

He has refused to pass other laws for the accommodation of large districts of people, unless those people would relinquish the right of representation in the legislature, a right inestimable to them and formidable to tyrants only.

He has called together legislative bodies at places unusual, uncomfortable and distant from the depository of their public records, for the sole purpose of fatiguing them into compliance with his measures.

He has dissolved representative houses repeatedly for opposing with manly firmness his invasions on the rights of the people.

He has refused for a long time, after such dissolutions, to cause others to be elected; whereby the legislative powers incapable of annihilation have returned to the people at large for their exercise; the state remaining in the meantime exposed to all the dangers of invasion from without and convulsions within.

He has endeavored to prevent the population of these states; for that purpose obstructing the laws for naturalization of foreigners; refusing to pass others to encourage their migrations hither & raising the conditions of new appropriations of lands.

He has obstructed the administration of Justice by refusing his assent to laws for establishing judiciary powers.

He has made judges dependent on his will alone for the tenure of their offices and the amount and payment of their salaries.

He has erected a multitude of new offices, and sent hither swarms of officers to harass our people and eat out their substance.

✓ He has kept among us in times of peace standing armies, without the consent of our legislatures.

He has affected to render the military independent of & superior to the civil power.

He has combined with others to subject us to a jurisdiction foreign to our constitution and unacknowledged by our laws, giving his assent to their acts of pretended legislation

    ، for quartering large bodies of troops[1] among us;

     for protecting them by a mock trial from punish-

[1] All other copies read "armed troops." Hazelton, *The Declaration of Independence*, 321.

ment for any murders, which they should commit on the inhabitants of these states.

for cutting off our trade with all parts of the world;

for imposing taxes on us without our consent;

for depriving us in many cases of the benefits of trial by jury;

for transporting us beyond seas to be tried for pretended offences;

for abolishing the free system of english laws in a neighboring province, establishing therein an arbitrary government and enlarging its boundaries, so as to render it at once an example & fit instrument for introducing the same absolute rule into these colonies.

for taking away our charters, abolishing our most valuable laws and altering fundamentally the forms of our governments.

for suspending our own legislatures and declaring themselves invested with power to legislate for us in all cases whatsoever.

He has abdicated government here by declaring us out of his protection and waging war against us.

He has plundered our seas, ravaged our coasts burnt our towns & destroyed the lives of our people.

He is at this time transporting large armies of foreign mercenaries to compleat the works of death, desolation and tyranny, already begun with circumstances of cruelty and perfidy scarcely paralleled in the most barbarous ages and totally unworthy the head of a civilized nation.

He has constrained our fellow citizens taken captive on the high seas to bear arms against their country, to become the executioners of their freinds and brethren or to fall themselves by their hands.

He has excited domestic insurrections amongst us and has endeavoured to bring on the inhabitants of our frontiers the merciless indian savages, whose known rule of warfare is an undistinguished destruction of all ages, sexes and conditions.

Such were the 'facts' submitted to a candid world. It is important to note that they were not submitted as being, in themselves, a justification for rebellion; they were submitted to prove that the deliberate and persistent purpose of the king was to establish an 'absolute tyranny' over the colonies. A most significant thing about this long list of the king's alleged actions is the assumption that in each case the king acted with deliberate intention and from a bad motive. It is the bad general purpose of the king, rather than his bad particular acts, that makes the indictment so effective. And this effect is enhanced by the form in which the 'facts' are presented — the steady, laborious piling up of 'facts,' the monotonous enumeration, without comment, of one bad action after another. How could a candid world deny that the colonies were rightly absolved from allegiance to so malevolent a will!

Nevertheless, in spite of multiplied and long continued grievances, the colonies had not rushed into rebellion.

In every stage of these oppressions we have petitioned for redress in the most humble terms: Our repeated petitions have been answered only by repeated injury. A prince whose character is thus marked by every act, which may define a tyrant, is unfit to be the ruler of a free people.

Nor have we been wanting in attentions to our british brethren. We have warned them from time to time of attempts by their legislature to extend an unwarrantable jurisdiction over us. We have reminded them of the circumstances of our emigration and settlement here. We have appealed to their native justice and magnanimity and we have conjured them by the ties of our common kindred to disavow these usurpations, which would inevitably interrupt our connections & correspondence. They too have been deaf to the voice of justice & consanguinity.[1] We must therefore acquiesce in the necessity, which denounces our separation, and hold them, as we hold the rest of mankind, enemies in war, in peace friends.

Thus the framers of the Declaration presented their case. Having formulated a philosophy of government which made revolution right under certain conditions, they endeavored to show that these conditions prevailed in the colonies, not on account of anything which the people of the colonies had done, or had left undone, but solely on account of the deliberate and malevolent purpose of their king to establish over them an 'absolute tyranny.' The people of the colonies must, accordingly (such is the implication), either throw off the yoke or submit to be slaves. As between these alternatives, there could be but one choice for men accustomed to freedom.

We therefore the representatives of the united States of America in general Congress assembled appealing to the supreme judge of the world for the rectitude of our inten-

---

[1] All other copies read "of consanguinity." *Ibid.*, 335.

tions do in the name and by authority of the good people of these colonies solemnly publish and declare —

That these united colonies are and of right ought to be free and independent States; that they are absolved from all allegiance to the british Crown, and that all political connection between them and the state of great Britain is & ought to be totally dissolved; and that as free & independent states they have full power to levy war, conclude peace, contract alliances, establish commerce, and to do all other acts & things, which independent states may of right do. And for the support of this declaration, with a firm reliance on the protection of divine providence, we mutually pledge to each other our lives, our fortunes & our sacred honor.

From the foregoing analysis it is clear that, apart from the preamble and the conclusion, the Declaration consists of two parts, apparently quite distinct. The first part is contained in the second paragraph. In these few lines the Declaration formulates, in general terms, a democratic political philosophy. The second and much longer part of the Declaration enumerates the specific grievances against the king of Great Britain, which, ostensibly, are presented as the historical causes of the Revolution. These two parts of the Declaration, apparently quite distinct, are nevertheless intimately related in the logic and purpose of the Declaration. Superficially, the Declaration seems chiefly concerned with the causes of the Revolution, with the specific grievances; but in reality it is chiefly, one might say solely, concerned with a theory of government — with a theory of government in general, and a theory of the British empire in particular. The theory of government in general is explicitly formulated; the theory of the British empire is not explicitly formulated but is implicitly taken for granted; and the second part of the Declaration was carefully phrased so that no assertion or implication might appear as a contradiction or a denial of the assumed theory.

The Declaration thus bcomes interesting for what it omits as well as for what it includes. For example, it does not, in its final form, contain the word 'Parliament' — a most significant omission, considering that the controversy of the preceding decade was occasioned, not by the acts of the king, who plays the leading part in the Declaration, but by the acts of the British Parliament. In all the controversy leading up to the Revolution the thing chiefly debated was the authority of the British Parliament. What is the nature, and what precisely are the limits, of the authority of the British Parliament over the colonies? This question was in fact the central issue. Nevertheless, the Declaration does not mention the British Parliament.

So striking an omission must have been intentional. It was of course impossible to make out a list of grievances against Great Britain without referring to such acts as the Stamp Act, the Declaratory Act, the Boston Port Bill, and many other legislative measures; and the framers of the Declaration, when they brought these measures into the indictment, had accordingly to resort to circumlocution in order to avoid naming the Parliament that passed them. There are, in the Declaration, two such veiled references to the Parliament. The first is this: "He [the king] has combined with others to subject us to a jurisdiction foreign to our constitution and unacknowledged by our laws, giving his assent to their pretended acts of legislation." These 'others' who have passed pretended acts of legislation are the members of the British Parliament. The second reference is this: "We have warned them [our british brethren] . . . of attempts by their legislature to extend an unwarrantable jurisdiction over us." Obviously, the framers of the Declaration make it a point of principle not on any account to pronounce the word Parliament. "Of course," we seem to hear them saying, " our British brethren have their legislature, as we have ours. But with their legislature we have nothing to do, God forbid! The very name of the thing escapes us! At least, let us pretend so."

Another significant omission is the term 'rights of British subjects.' Throughout the controversy the colonists had commonly protested against parliamentary taxation precisely on the ground that they possessed the rights of British subjects. They said that the British Parliament could not constitutionally tax British subjects without their consent, and that British subjects in the colonies were not, and in the nature of the case could not well be, represented in the British Parliament. For ten years the colonists had made the 'rights of British subjects' the very foundation of their case. Yet this is just what the framers of the Declaration carefully refrain from doing: the term 'rights of British subjects' does not appear in the Declaration. Trial by jury is mentioned, but not as a right of British subjects. 'The system of free English laws' is mentioned, but it is not stated, or even implied, that the validity of these laws arises from the fact that they are English laws. Nowhere does the Declaration

say, and [nowhere does it imply, that the acts of
the king are intolerable because they violate
the rights of British subjects.]

The framers of the Declaration refrained from
mentioning Parliament and the 'rights of British
subjects' for the same reason that they charged
all their grievances against the king alone.
Being now committed to independence, the
position of the colonies could not be simply
or convincingly presented from the point of
view of the rights of British subjects. To have
said: 'We hold this truth to be self-evident,
that it is a right of British subjects not to be
taxed except by their own consent,' would
have made no great appeal to mankind, since
mankind in general could not be supposed to
be vitally interested in the rights of British
subjects, or much disposed to regard them as
axioms in political speculation.] Separation from
Great Britain was therefore justified on more
general grounds, on the ground of the natural
rights of man; and in order to simplify the
issue, in order to make it appear that the rights
of man had been undeniably and flagrantly
violated, it was expedient that these rights
should seem to be as little as possible limited
or obscured by the positive and legal obligations
that were admittedly binding upon British
subjects. To place the Resolution of Independ-

ence in the best light possible, it was convenient to assume that the connection between the colonies and Great Britain had never been a very close connection, never, strictly speaking, a connection binding in positive law, but only a connection voluntarily entered into by a free people. On this ground the doctrine of the rights of man would have a free field and no competitors.

The specific grievances enumerated in the Declaration were accordingly presented from the point of view of a carefully considered and resolutely held constitutional theory of the British empire. The essence of this theory, nowhere explicitly formulated in the Declaration, but throughout implicitly taken for granted, is that the colonies became parts of the empire by their own voluntary act, and remained parts of it solely by virtue of a compact subsisting between them and the king. Their rights were those of all men, of every free people; their obligations such as a free people might incur by professing allegiance to the personal head of the empire. On this theory, both the Parliament and the rights of British subjects could be ignored as irrelevant to the issue.

The specific grievances complained of in the Declaration are grievances no longer. As concrete issues they are happily dead. But the way in which the men of those days conceived of these concrete issues, the intellectual preconceptions, illusions if you like, which were born of their hopes and fears, and which in turn shaped their conduct — these make the Declaration always interesting and worthy of study. It is not my intention to search out those particular measures of the British government which served in the mind of Jefferson and his friends to validate each particular charge against the king. This could indeed be done, and has been sufficiently done already; but the truth is that when one has found the particular act to which in each case the particular charge was intended to refer, one is likely to think the poor king less malevolently guilty than he is made out to be. Yet that Jefferson and his friends, honest and good men enough, and more intelligent than most, were convinced that the Declaration was a true bill, we need not doubt. How this could be may be understood, a little at least, by seeing how the pressure of circumstances enabled the men of those days to accept as true their general philosophy of human rights and their particular theory of the British empire.

CHAPTER II

HISTORICAL ANTECEDENTS OF THE DEC-
LARATION: THE NATURAL RIGHTS
PHILOSOPHY

WHETHER the political philosophy of the
Declaration of Independence is "true" or
"false" has been much discussed. In the late
eighteenth century it was widely accepted as
a commonplace. At a later time, in 1822,
John Adams made this a ground for detracting
from the significance of Jefferson's share in the
authorship of the famous document. He was
perhaps a little irritated by the laudation which
Fourth of July orators were lavishing on his
friend, and wished to remind his countrymen
that others had had a hand in the affair. "There
is not an idea in it," he wrote to Pickering,
"but what had been hackneyed in Congress
for two years before."[1] This is substantially
true; but as a criticism, if it was intended as
such, it is wholly irrelevant, since the strength
of the Declaration was precisely that it said
what everyone was thinking. Nothing could

[1] *Works of John Adams*, II, 512.

24

have been more futile than an attempt to justify a revolution on principles which no one had ever heard of before.

In replying to Adams' strictures, Jefferson had only to state this simple fact.

Pickering's observations, and Mr. Adams' in addition, that it contained no new ideas, that it is a commonplace compilation, its sentiments hacknied in Congress for two years before . . . may all be true. Of that I am not to be the judge. Richard H. Lee charged it as copied from Locke's treatise on Government. . . . I know only that I turned to neither book nor pamphlet while writing it. I did not consider it as any part of my charge to invent new ideas altogether and to offer no sentiment which had ever been expressed before.[1]

In writing to Lee, in 1825, Jefferson said again that he only attempted to express the ideas of the Whigs, who all thought alike on the subject. The essential thing was

Not to find out new principles, or new arguments, never before thought of, not merely to say things which had never been said before; but to place before mankind the common sense of the subject, in terms so plain and firm

[1] *The writings of Thomas Jefferson* (Ed. 1869), VII, 304.

as to command their assent. . . . Neither aiming at originality of principles or sentiments, nor yet copied from any particular and previous writing, it was intended to be an expression of the American mind. . . . All its authority rests then on the harmonizing sentiments of the day, whether expressed in conversation, in letters, printed essays, or the elementary books of public right,⟩ as Aristotle, Cicero, Locke, Sidney, etc.[1]

Not all Americans, it is true, would have accepted the philosophy of the Declaration, just as Jefferson phrased it, without qualification, as the 'common sense of the subject'; but one may say that the premises of this philosophy, the underlying preconceptions from which it is derived, were commonly taken for granted. That there is a 'natural order' of things in the world, cleverly and expertly designed by God for the guidance of mankind; that the 'laws' of this natural order may be discovered by human reason; that these laws so discovered furnish a reliable and immutable standard for testing the ideas, the conduct, and the institutions of men — these were the accepted premises, the preconceptions, of most eighteenth century thinking, not only in America but also

[1] *Ibid.*, 407.

in England and France. They were, as Jefferson says, the 'sentiments of the day, whether expressed in conversation, in letters, printed essays, or the elementary books of public right.' Where Jefferson got his ideas is hardly so much a question as where he could have got away from them.

Since these sentiments of the day were common in France, and were most copiously, and perhaps most logically, expressed there, it has sometimes been thought that Jefferson and his American contemporaries must have borrowed their ideas from French writers, must have been 'influenced' by them, for example by Rousseau. But it does not appear that Jefferson, or any American, read many French books. So far as the 'Fathers' were, before 1776, directly influenced by particular writers, the writers were English, and notably Locke. (Most Americans had absorbed Locke's works as a kind of political gospel;) and the Declaration, in its form, in its phraseology, follows closely certain sentences in Locke's second treatise on government. This is interesting, but it does not tell us why Jefferson, having read Locke's treatise, was so taken with it that he read it again, and still again, so that afterwards its very phrases reappear in his own writing. Jefferson doubtless read Filmer as well as Locke; but the phrases of Filmer, happily, do not appear in the Declaration. Generally speaking, men are influenced by books which clarify their own thought, which express their own notions well, or which suggest to them ideas which their minds are already predisposed to accept. If Jefferson had read Rousseau's *Social Contract* we may be sure he would have been strongly impressed by it. What has to be explained is why the best minds of the eighteenth century were so ready to be impressed by Locke's treatise on civil government and by Rousseau's *Social Contract*. What we have to seek is the origin of those common underlying preconceptions that made the minds of many men, in different countries, run along the same track in their political thinking.

It is well known that Locke's treatise, written in reply to Filmer's *Patriarcha*, was an apology for the Revolution of 1688. "Kings," said Filmer, "are as absolute as Adam over the creatures"; and in general the Stuart partisans had taken their stand, as Sir Frederick Pollock says, "on a supposed indefeasible right of kings, derived from a supposed divine institution of monarchy. . . . The Whigs needed an antidote, and Locke found one in his modified version of the original compact."[1] This means

---

[1] *History of the Science of Politics*, 65.

that political circumstances had brought the
Whigs to the point of overturning the existing government, that they were human enough
to wish to feel that this was a decent and right
thing to do, and that, accordingly, their minds
were disposed to welcome a reasoned theory
of politics which would make their revolution,
as a particular example under the general rule,
respectable and meritorious. The Whigs needed
a theory of politics that would make their revolution of 1688 a 'glorious revolution.' Locke
said himself that he had made all his discoveries
by "steadily intending his mind in a given
direction." Inevitably the Whigs steadily 'intended their minds' away from the idea of a
divine right in kings, since no glorious revolution
was to be found there, and towards a new
idea — in fact, towards Locke's modified version of the compact theory.

It is significant that English writers were
formulating a new version of the compact theory
in the seventeenth century, while French and
American writers made little use of it until the
late eighteenth century. This does not necessarily mean that British writers were more
intelligent and up-to-date, but is probably due
to the fact that in British history the seventeenth
century was the time of storm and stress for
kings, whereas this time fell later in France and

America. Jefferson used the compact theory to justify revolution just as Locke did: the theory came with the revolution in both cases. Rousseau was indeed not justifying an actual revolution; but, as Chateaubriand said, the Revolution in France "was accomplished before it occurred." It was accomplished in men's minds before they made it the work of their hands; and Rousseau spoke for all those who were 'intending their minds' away from an actual, irrational, and oppressive political order which rested in theory upon the divine right of kings and priests to rule — and misrule. In all three countries this common influence — the widespread desire to limit the power of kings and priests — was one source of those underlying presuppositions which determined the character of political speculation in the eighteenth century; a strong antipathy to kings and priests predisposed Jefferson and Rousseau, as it predisposed Locke, to 'intend their minds' towards some new sanction for political authority.

The idea that secular political authority rested upon compact was not new — far from it; and it had often enough been used to limit the authority of princes. It could scarcely have been otherwise indeed in that feudal age in which the mutual obligations of vassal and

overlord were contractually conceived and defined. Vassals were often kings and kings
often vassals; but all were manifestly vassals
of God who was the Lord of lords and the King
of kings. Thus mediaeval philosophers had
conceived of the authority of princes as resting upon a compact with their subjects, a
compact on their part to rule righteously,
failing which their subjects were absolved from
allegiance; but this absolution was commonly
thought to become operative only through the
intervention of the Pope, who, as the Vice-
gerent of God on earth, possessed by divine
right authority over princes as well as over
other men. Thus princes ruled by divine
right after all, only their right was a second
hand right, deriving from God through the
Pope. Afterwards the princes, when they had
become kings and as kings had got the upper
hand, jostled the Pope out of his special seat
and became coequals with him in God's favor;
so that in the seventeenth century the right of
kings to rule was commonly thought to come
directly from God, and the Pope lost his power
of intervening to absolve subjects from allegiance to a bad king. Charles II of England
and Louis XIV of France both thought this a
reasonable doctrine, nor did either of them lack
learned men to back them up; Bossuet proved

that it was obviously good religious doctrine — *Politique tirée de l'Écriture Sainte;* while Cambridge University assured Charles II that "Kings derive not their authority from the people but from God; . . . To Him only they are accountable."[1]

This clearly closed the door to relief in case there should be any bad kings. In the sixteenth and seventeenth centuries there were a number of bad kings; and so some people were always to be found seeking a method of bringing bad kings to book. ⟨Popular resistance to kings was commonly taught both by the Jesuits and the Protestant dissenters: by the Jesuits (by Catholic monarchists called "dissenters") on the ground that only the Pope has Divine authority; by Protestant Dissenters (by Protestant monarchists called "Jesuits") on the ground that it was possible for subjects themselves to claim as intimate relations with God as either king or Pope. Calvin was one of the writers who opened up this latter inviting prospect to suceeding generations.

The first duty of subjects towards their rulers is to entertain the most honorable views of their office, recognizing it [the office not the king] as a delegated jurisdiction

---

[1] *History of Passive Obedience,* 108.

from God, and on that account receiving and reverencing them as the ministers and ambassadors of God.

This is admitted; but then the ambassador must clearly abide by his instructions; and therefore,

In that obedience which we hold to be due to the commands of rulers we must . . . be particularly careful that it is not incompatible with obedience to Him to whose will the wishes of all kings should be subject. . . . The Lord, therefore, is King of Kings. . . . We are subject to men who rule over us, but subject only in the Lord. If they command anything against Him, let us not pay the least heed to it.[1]

What God had commanded, subjects might plainly read in holy writ — the scriptures as interpreted by those ministers whose business it was to understand them; for which reason, no doubt, Calvin would have ministers and magistrates walk together in close communion.

In 1579, another Frenchman, Hubert Languet, or whoever it was that wrote the *Vindiciae contra tyrannos*, gave greater precision to this idea. Subjects are obviously not bound to obey a king who commands what is contrary

----

[1] *Institutes of Christianity*, Bk. IV, Ch. 20, sec. 22, 32.

to the will of God. But are they bound to
resist such a king? According to the *Vindiciae*
they are. When kings were set up, two compacts were entered into: in the first, God on
the one side, and people and king on the other,
engaged to maintain the ancient covenant which
God had formerly made with his chosen people
of Israel; in the second, the king contracted
with his subjects to rule justly, and they with
him to be obedient.[1] Thus kings are under
binding contract to rule justly, while subjects
have a covenant with God to see that they do
so. In the seventeenth century English sec-
taries not only preached but practiced resistance
to kings and magistrates, finding their justification, not so much in an explicit compact
with God, as in natural law, which was that
right reason or inner light of conscience which
God had given to men for their guidance. The
Levellers were complained of because, be the
"Lawes and customes of a Kingdom never so
plain and cleer against their wayes, yet they
will not submit, but cry out for natural rights
derived from Adam and right reason." Milton
spoke for the refractory dissenters of that age
when he said,

There is no power but of God (Paul, *Rom.* 13), as much
as to say, God put it in man's heart to find out that way

---

[1] *Vindiciae contra tyrannos* (ed. 1579), 55.

at first for common peace and preservation, approving the exercise thereof. . . . For if it needs must be a sin in them to depose, it may as likely be a sin to have elected. And contrary, if the people's act in election be pleaded by a king, as the act of God and the most just title to enthrone him, why may not the people's act of rejection be as well pleaded by the people as the act of God, and the most just reason to depose him?[1]

Here was a 'version of the original compact' which Locke might have used to justify the Revolution of 1688. He might have said, with any amount of elaboration, that the people had a compact with God which reserved to them the right to rebel when kings ruled unrighteously. Why was Locke not satisfied with this version? Certainly no one had less desire than Locke to deny that God was the maker and ruler of all. He could quote scripture too, as well as Milton or Filmer. We see, he says, that in the dispute between Jephthah and the Ammonites, "he [Jephthah] was forced to appeal to Heaven: "The Lord the Judge (says he) be judge this day." Well, of course, says Locke, "everyone knows what Jephthah here tells us, that the

[1] "Tenure of Kings and Magistrates"; *Works of John Milton* (Mitford ed., 1851), IV, 464, 465.

Lord the Judge shall judge."[1] But the trouble is the Lord does not do it now; he reserves his decision till the Day of Judgment. Jephthah appealed to the Lord, but the Lord did not speak, did not decide the dispute between Jephthah and the Ammonites; the result of which was that Jephthah had to decide it himself by leading out his armies. So it always is in the affairs of men: whether I shall appeal to Heaven, "I myself can only be the judge in my own conscience, as I will answer it, at the great day, to the supreme judge of all men." If we resist kings, God will no doubt judge us for it in the last day; but men will judge us now. Let us, therefore, ask whether there is not happily a compact between men and kings, God not interfering, on which we can stand to be judged by men when we resist kings.

The truth is that Locke, and the English Whigs, and Jefferson and Rousseau even more so, had lost that sense of intimate intercourse and familiar conversation with God which religious men of the sixteenth and seventeenth centuries enjoyed. Since the later seventeenth century, God had been withdrawing from immediate contact with men, and had become, in proportion as he receded into the dim distance,

---

[1] "Of Civil Government," Bk. II, sec. 21; *Works of John Locke* (ed. 1812), V, 350.

no more than the Final Cause, or Great Contriver, or Prime Mover of the universe; and as
such was conceived as exerting his power and
revealing his will indirectly through his creation
rather than directly by miraculous manifesta-
tion or through inspired books. In the eighteenth century as never before, 'Nature' had
stepped in between man and God; so that there
was no longer any way to know God's will
except by discovering the 'laws' of Nature,
which would doubtless be the laws of 'nature's
god' as Jefferson said. "Why should I go in
search of Moses to find out what God has said to
Jean Jacques Rousseau?" Why indeed, when
the true revelation was all about him in Nature,
with sermons in stones, books in the running
brooks, and God in everything. The eighteenth
century, seeking a modified version of the
original compact, had to find it in nature or
forever abandon the hope of finding it.

The concept of Nature was of course nothing
new either, any more than the theory of compact. Stoic philosophers and Roman jurists
had made much of Nature and Natural Law.
Thomas Aquinas, in the thirteenth century,
noted three distinct meanings of the word
natural as applied to man. The third of these
meanings, which mediaeval writers had taken
over from the classical world, Aquinas defines

as "an inclination in man to the good, according to the *rational* nature which is proper to him; as, for example, man has a natural inclination to know the truth about God, and to live in society." Natural law was accordingly that part of law discoverable by right reason, and as such occupied a strictly subordinate place in the mediaeval hierarchy of laws. According to Aquinas, the highest of all laws, comprehending all others, was the Eternal Law, which was nothing less than the full mind of God. Something, but not all, of the mind of God could be known to man: part of it had been revealed in the Bible or might be communicated through the Church (Positive Divine Law); and part of it could be discovered by human reason (Natural Law); lowest of all in the hierarchy came Human Law, or the positive laws of particular states.[1]   Thus Natural Law obviously took precedence over Human Law, but must always be subordinate to that part of the Eternal Law which God had revealed in the Bible or through the Church. Natural Law was in fact not the law of nature, but a natural method of learning about the law of God. Above all, what could be learned by this method was strictly limited: Natural Law was that part of the mind of God which man could discover by using his

[1] Quoted in Richie, *Natural Rights*, 39.

reason, but God had provided beforehand, through the Bible and the Church, a sure means of letting man know when his reason was not right reason but unreason.

The concept of Nature which held the field in the eighteenth century seems at first sight very different from this; but the difference is after all mainly on the surface. The eighteenth century did not abandon the old effort to share in the mind of God; it only went about it with greater confidence, and had at last the presumption to think that the infinite mind of God and the finite mind of man were one and the same thing. This complacent view of the matter came about partly through the Protestant Reformation, which did much to diminish the authority of the Church as the official interpreter of God's will; but it came about still more through the progress of scientific investigation which had been creating, since the time of Copernicus, a strong presumption that the mind of God could be made out with greater precision by studying the mechanism of his created universe than by meditating on the words of his inspired prophets. Some of the 'laws' of this curious mechanism had already been formulated by Kepler and Galileo. Well, what if all the 'laws' of God's universe could be discovered by the human reason? In that case

would not the infinite mind of God be fully
revealed, and the Natural Law be identical with
the Eternal Law? Descartes was bold enough to
suggest this wonderful possibility. "I think,
therefore, I am." Whatever is, is rational;
hence there is an exact correspondence between
human reason and the objective world. I
think, therefore I am; and if I can think straight
enough and far enough, I can identify myself
with all that is. This 'all that is' the eighteenth
century understood as Nature; and to effect
a rational explanation of the relation and operation of all that is, was what it meant by discovering the 'laws' of Nature. No doubt Natural
Law was still, as in the time of Aquinas, that
part of the mind of God which a rational creature
could comprehend; but (if a rational creature
could comprehend all that God had done, it
would, for all practical purposes, share completely the mind of God, and the Natural Law
would be, in the last analysis, identical with the
Eternal Law.) Having deified Nature, the eighteenth century could conveniently dismiss the
Bible and drop the concept of Eternal Law
altogether.

In this deification of Nature, a decisive influence must be ascribed to Isaac Newton, whose
great work, the *Principia*, was first published
in 1686. Newton probably had no intention

of deifying Nature. He was engaged in more commonplace occupations: noting the effect which an ordinary glass prism had upon rays of light which passed through it; determining whether the deflection of the moon's orbit, in any minute of the moon's progress, was the same as the distance which a body at that height would move in the first minute of its fall towards the earth. But Newton struck the imagination of his time, as Darwin did of his time, just because his important conclusions were arrived at by such commonplace methods. If the character of so intangible a thing as light could be discovered by playing with a prism, if, by looking through a telescope and doing a sum in mathematics, the force which held the planets could be identified with the force that made an apple fall to the ground, there seemed to be no end to what might be definitely known about the universe. Perhaps after all God moved in these clear ways to perform his wonders; and it must be that he had given man a mind ingeniously fitted to discover these ways. Newton, more than any man before him, so it seemed to the eighteenth century, banished mystery from the world. In his hands 'Philosophy' came to be no more than a matter of observation and mathematics, an occupation which any intelligent person might in some measure pursue, instead of the manipulation of a subtle dialectic which only the adept could follow and which created more difficulties than it solved.

The interest of the scientific world in Newton's work is indicated by the appearance, prior to 1789, of some eighteen editions or reprintings of the *Principia*.[1]   British universities were teaching the new doctrine before the end of the seventeenth century; and when Newton, crowned with honors and offices, died in 1727, his funeral was a national event, observed with forms usually accorded only to royalty.   At that time Descartes was still in the ascendant in France.   Newton was not indeed unknown there, having been admitted, as early as 1699, to the small number of foreign associates of the Academy of Sciences; but it was not until after his death that his doctrines were much attended to in France.   In 1734, the annual prize of the Academy was shared by John Bernoulli, who had submitted a Cartesian memoir, and his son Daniel, who had defended the Newtonian theories.   The last prize granted for a Cartesian paper was in 1740.   Voltaire, who was in England at the time of Newton's death, came home and devoted himself to con-

[1] Gray, G. J. *A Bibliography of the Works of Sir Isaac Newton.* 2nd ed. Cambridge, 1907.

vincing his countrymen that they were be-
hind the times in still holding to Descartes, for
that purpose preparing the very influential
book of exposition, *Elemens de la philosophie
de Newton*, which was published in 1738.
Fontenelle, the most distinguished defender of
Cartesianism in France, died in 1756; and by
1759, when the *Principia* appeared in a French
translation, it may be said that French sci-
entists had generally accepted the Newtonian
philosophy.[1]

But the fame of Newton was not confined to
the scientific fraternity. It was not necessary
to read the *Principia* in order to be a good
Newtonian, any more than it is necessary to
read the *Origin of Species* in order to be a good
Darwinian. Relatively few people read the
Principia, which contains much difficult mathematics. No less a person than Dr. Richard
Bentley wrote to Newton for a list of books
on mathematics by the aid of which he could
study the *Principia* intelligently; and John
Locke, himself no mean philosopher, had to
take the word of Huygens that the mathematical
parts of the book were sound.[2] "Very few
people read Newton," said Voltaire, ' because it

---

[1] Wheewell, *History of the Inductive Sciences*, I, 421 ff. Gray,
op. cit.

[2] Brewster, D. *Memoirs of Sir Isaac Newton*, I, 339, 340.

is necessary to be learned to understand him. But everybody talks about him." [1]   These people could subscribe to the Newtonian philosophy without ever having to open the formidable *Principia;* and they were well aware that the great scientist had uncovered the secrets of Nature, and of Nature's God, in a way that, to an earlier generation, might have seemed almost indiscreet.   They were indoctrinated into the new philosophy through conversation, and through popular lectures and books which humanely omitted the mathematics of the *Principia*, devoting the space thus gained to a confident and edifying amplification of its cautious conclusions which might have astonished Sir Isaac himself, but which made the new philosophy interesting and important to the average man.

The number of such books of popularization was, relatively speaking, very great.   In Mr. Gray's admirable bibliography one may count, among the books about the *Principia* published before 1789, 40 in English, 17 in French, 3 in German, 11 in Latin, 1 in Portuguese, and 1 in Italian.   This does not include books about the other works of Newton, such as the *Optics;* nor does it include separate editions of the books enumerated above, of which, in the case

---

[1] "Lettres philosophiques," XIV; *Oeuvres* (ed. 1879), XXII, 130.

of the most popular works, there were sometimes a half dozen or more. For example, in 1720 J. T. Desaguliers published a two-volume translation of 's Gravesande's Latin work, *Physices elementa mathematica*, under the title, *Mathematical Elements of Natural Philosophy, confirmed by Experiments; or an Introduction to Sir Isaac Newton's Philosophy.* To meet the demand for this book a one-volume edition was issued the following year; while a fourth edition appeared in 1731, and a sixth in 1747. Desaguliers evidently found a great deal in the Newtonian philosophy, more than Newton ever discovered; for we find him publishing, in 1728, *The Newtonian System of the World the Best Model of Government, an Allegorical Poem.*

Another successful popularizer was Benjamin Martin, who went about giving courses of lectures, with experiments. The ladies and gentlemen who paid their money for this new learning, finding some difficulties, petitioned Mr. Martin, so at least he tells us, "to draw up such an Introduction to Philosophy as might prepare them to understand the several subjects of my lectures and experiments, and when these are over to refresh their memories." What they wanted was' an easy textbook; and their "constant importunity" induced Mr. Martin, in 1751, to publish such a book:

A Plain and Familiar Introduction to the Newtonian Philosophy in Six Lectures.   Illustrated by Six Copper Plates.   Designed for the use of such Gentlemen and Ladies as would acquire a competent Knowledge of this Science without Mathematical Learning; and more especially those who have or may attend the Author's Course of Six Lectures and Experiments on these subjects.

The demand for this celebrated work was such that five editions were printed within fifteen years.   Besides, it was not alone in the field. James Ferguson's *Astronomy Explained upon Newton's Principles, and made easy to those who have not studied mathematics,* first published in 1756, went into the seventh edition in 1773. Voltaire's *Elemens de la philosophie de Neuton,* 'revised and corrected,' was translated into English by John Hanna and published the same year it appeared in the original (1738). Nor were the ladies barred from the new philosophy.   Mr. Martin's lectures were designed for 'gentlemen and ladies'; and in 1737 Count Alogrotti published, at Naples, *Il Newtonianismo per le dame,* of which there were successive editions in 1738, 1739, and 1746.   The work was translated into French in 1738 (*Le newtonianisme pour les dames*), and into English in 1739 (*Theory of Light and Colours*), with new editions of the latter in 1742 and 1745.

In the hands of the popularizers, the Newtonian philosophy became a 'Philosophy' indeed: was broadened out into a 'System of the World' which could be made to serve as a model of government, an argument to confound atheists and 'libertines,' a sure mathematical foundation for natural religion, or a major premise from which a strictly materialistic interpretation could be derived. It was these broader uses of the Newtonian philosophy that made it so popular, and that gave to the work of Newton a significance beyond the narrow field of physics and astronomy. In truth Newton's name and fame played much the same part in eighteenth century thought which the name and fame of Darwin have played in the thought of our own day. His name became a symbol which called up, in the mind of the reading and thinking public, a generalized conception of the universe, a kind of philosophical premise of the most general type, one of those uncriticized preconceptions which so largely determined the social and political as well as the strictly scientific thinking of the age.

This generalized conception of the universe, through which the work of Newton so powerfully affected the social and political thought of the eighteenth century, is very clearly formulated by M. Leon Bloch, a competent modern student, in his recent book, *La philosophie de Newton.*

What the human spirit owes to Newton . . . is the *rapprochement* effected by this great man between God and nature. Henceforth it will be possible for natural science, that is to say physics, not only to struggle against theology, but to supplant it. The contradictory Gods of the revealed religions will be replaced by a new idea, that of a being who is known to us through his works, and to whom we can attain only through science. The universal order, symbolized henceforth by the law of gravitation, takes on a clear and positive meaning. This order is accessible to the mind, it is not preestablished mysteriously, it is the most evident of all facts. From this it follows that the sole reality which can be accessible to our means of knowledge, matter, nature, appears to us as a tissue of properties, precisely ordered, and of which the connection can be expressed in terms of mathematics.[1]

This is very neatly put, perhaps too neatly. We may, however, find much the same idea, less

[1] Bloch, L. *La Philosophie de Newton,* 555.

neatly put, put more in the English way, and with more of the eighteenth century flavor, in a contemporary work, *An Account of Sir Isaac Newton's Philosophical Discoveries*, by Colin Maclaurin. This was perhaps the·most substantial of the British works of exposition, yet sufficiently popular to run to three editions. Maclaurin was the most distinguished scientific disciple of Newton, a professor of mathematics in the University of Edinburgh. His exposition of Newton's experiments is doubtless correct enough, yet he does not hesitate to deduce from these experiments a general philosophy of the universe, in which the relation of God to Nature, and of man to both, is dogmatically expounded.

To describe the phenomena of nature, to explain their causes, to trace the relation and dependence of these causes, and to inquire into the whole constitution of the universe, is the business of Natural Philosophy. A strong curiosity has prompted men in all times to study nature; every useful art has some connection with this science; and the inexhaustible beauty and variety of things makes it even agreeable, new, and surprising.

But Natural Philosophy is subservient to purposes of a higher kind, and is chiefly to be valued as it lays a sure foundation for Natural Religion and Moral Philosophy; by leading us, in a satisfactory manner, to the knowledge of the Author and Governor of the universe. . . .

We are, from His works, to seek to know God, and not to pretend to mark out the scheme of His conduct, in nature, from the very different ideas we are able to form of that great mysterious Being. . . .

To study Nature is to study into His workmanship; every new discovery opens up to us a new part of His scheme. . . .

We may also learn . . . to be less fond of perfect and finished schemes of Natural Philosophy; to be willing to stop where we find we are not in a position to proceed further; and to leave to posterity to make greater advances. . . . For we cannot doubt that Nature has discoveries in store for future times also. . . . By proceeding with due care, every age will add to the common stock of knowledge; the mysteries that still lie concealed in Nature may be gradually opened, arts will flourish and increase, mankind will improve, and appear more worthy of their situation in the universe, as they approach more towards a perfect knowledge of Nature. . . .

Our views of Nature, however imperfect, serve to represent to us, in the most sensible manner, that mighty power which prevails throughout, acting with a force and efficacy that appears to suffer no diminution from the greatest distances of space or intervals of time; and that wisdom which we see equally displayed in the exquisite structure and just motions of the greatest and subtilest parts. These, with perfect goodness, by which they are evidently directed, constitute the supreme object of the speculations of a philosopher; who, while he contemplates and admires so excellent a system, cannot but be himself excited and animated to correspond with the general harmony of Nature.[1]

The eighteenth century, obviously, did not cease to bow down and worship; it only gave another form and a new name to the object of worship: it deified Nature and denatured God. Since Nature was now the new God, source of all wisdom and righteousness, it was to Nature that the eighteenth century looked for guidance, from Nature that it expected to receive the tablets of the law; and it was just as necessary now as ever for the mind of the rational creature to share in the mind of this

[1] Maclaurin, C. *An Account of Sir Isaac Newton's Philosophical Discoveries*, 3, 4, 95.

new God, in order that his conduct, including
the 'positive laws of particular states,' might
conform to the universal purpose. The Philosopher, as Maclaurin says, 'while he contemplates and admires so excellent a System,
*cannot but be himself excited and animated to
correspond with the general harmony of Nature.'*
The words may be taken as a just expression of
the eighteenth century state of mind: on its
knees, with uplifted eyes contemplating and
admiring the Universal Order, it was excited
and animated to correspond with the general
harmony.

This was no doubt an inspiring idea, but certainly not a new one. Great and good men in
all ages had endeavored to correspond with the
general harmony. Formerly this was conceived as an endeavor to become one with God;
and for some centuries the approved method,
in Europe, was thought to be fasting and prayer,
the denial of the flesh, the renunciation of the
natural man. "Who shall deliver me from
the body of this death!" cried the saint. The
physical and material world was thought to be
a disharmony, a prison house, a muddy vesture
of decay, closing in and blinding the spirit so
that it could not enter into the harmony that
was God. But the eighteenth century, conceiving of God as known only through his

work, conceived of his work as itself a universal harmony, of which the material and the spiritual were but different aspects.

In breaking down the barriers between the material and the spiritual world, between man and nature, John Locke played a great rôle. His *Essay Concerning the Human Understanding*, published in 1690, was an enquiry into "the original, certainty, and extent of human knowledge," an enquiry which the author thought of the highest use "since it is the understanding that sets man above the rest of sensible beings, and gives him all the advantage and dominion which he has over them." The first part of this enquiry was devoted to 'ideas,' and 'how they come into the mind." On this point Locke thought he had something new to say, and his first task was to show how untenable the currently accepted view was.

It is an established opinion amongst some men, that there are in the *understanding* certain *innate principles,* some primary notions . . . stamped upon the mind of man, which the soul receives in its very first being, and brings into the world with it. It would be sufficient to convince unprejudiced readers of the falseness of this supposition, if I should only show . . . how men, barely by the use of their natural faculties, may attain to all the knowledge they have, without the help of any innate impressions. . . . For I imagine any one will easily grant that it would be impertinent to suppose the ideas of colours innate in a creature, to whom God hath given sight and power to receive them by the eyes, from external objects: and no less unreasonable would it be to attribute several truths to the impressions of nature, and innate characters, when we may observe in ourselves faculties fit to attain as easy and certain knowledge of them, as if they were originally imprinted on the mind.[1]

Although this alone, Locke thought, ought to convince a reasonable man, he nevertheless devoted sixty pages of fine print to proving that there is no such thing as an innate idea; and having demonstrated this point, he devoted more pages still to proving that "all ideas come from sensation or reflection."

Let us then suppose the mind to be, as we say, white paper, void of all characters, without any *ideas;* how comes it to be furnished? . . . To this I answer, in one word, from *experience;* in that all our knowledge is founded, and from that it ultimately derives itself. Our observation employed either about *external sensible*

[1] Locke, *Essay* (ed. 1813), I, 42.

objects, or about the internal operations of our minds, per-
ceived and reflected on by ourselves, is that which supplies
our understandings with all the materials of thinking.
These two are the fountains of knowledge, from which
all the ideas we have, or can naturally have, do spring.[1]

Of these two fountains of knowledge, the more
important was the first — impressions received
from external sensible objects. This "great
source of most of the ideas we have, depending
wholly upon our senses, and derived from them
to the understanding, I call SENSATION."

Locke's 'sensational' philosophy became, with
some modifications in detail, the psychological
gospel of the eighteenth century. A trained
philosopher might think that the conception of
'innate ideas' which Locke destroyed was no
more than a man of straw, a "theory of innate
ideas," as Mr. Webb says, "so crude that it is
difficult to suppose any serious thinker ever held
it."[2] That may be. Yet it is certain that
Locke's book had a great influence on the common thought of his age, which may be due to
the fact that serious thinkers are few, while
crude theories, generally speaking, rule the
world. Put in the form in which it entered

[1] *Ibid.*, 97, 98.
[2] Webb, C. J., *Studies in the History of Natural Theology*, 354.

into the common thought of the eighteenth century, Locke's theory may be stated as follows: God has not revealed the truth that is necessary for man's guidance, once for all, in holy writ, or stamped upon the minds of all men certain intuitively perceived intellectual and moral ideas which correspond to the truth so revealed; on the contrary, all the ideas we can have come from experience, are the result of the sensations that flow in upon us from the natural and social world without, and of the operations of the reflecting mind upon these sensations; from which it follows that man, as a thinking and an acting creature, is part and parcel of the world in which he lives, intimately and irrevocably allied to that Universal Order which is at once the work and the will of God.

Locke's *Essay Concerning the Human Understanding* went into the 26th edition in 1828. There is in existence a copy of this edition which contains an autograph letter from Andrew Lang to a friend: "Dear Grose, This is yours; I never read one word of Mr. Locke, but how did the dreary devil stagger like Crockett to a 26th edition?"[1] The answer to this question is that most of the twenty-six editions were printed in the eighteenth century, and the

---

[1] Autograph letter quoted in Sotheran's second-hand book catalogue, No. 61, p. 31.

eighteenth century prized Locke because he furnished a formal argument in support of the idea that "men, *barely by the use of their natural faculties*, may attain to all the knowledge they have." Locke, more perhaps than any one else, made it possible for the eighteenth century to believe what it wanted to believe: namely, that in the world of human relations as well as in the physical world, it was possible for men to 'correspond with the general harmony of Nature'; that since man, and the mind of man, were integral parts of the work of God, it was possible for man, by the use of his mind, to bring his thought and conduct, and hence the institutions by which he lived, into a perfect harmony with the Universal Natural Order. In the eighteenth century, therefore, these truths were widely accepted as self evident: that a valid morality would be a 'natural morality,' a valid religion would be a 'natural religion,' a valid law of politics would be a 'natural law.' This was only another way of saying that morality, religion, and politics ought to conform to God's will as revealed in the essential nature of man.

It went without saying that kings and ministers and priests, as well as philosophers, ought to be 'excited and animated to correspond with the general harmony of Nature'; and if, once fully enlightened on that point, they would not do so, they must unquestionably be pronounced no better than rebels against the Great Contriver, the Author and Governor of the Universe. But how, after all, could you tell for sure whether kings and ministers and priests were, or were not, in accord with Nature? The presumption was no doubt against them, but how be sure? In appealing from custom and positive law to the over-ruling law of God, the eighteenth century followed well established precedent; but a practical difficulty arose when the will of God was thought to be revealed, neither in papal command nor in the words of scripture, but in the endless, half-deciphered Book of Nature. Nature was doubtless an open book, yet difficult to read, and likely to convey many meanings, so various a language did it speak. George III, as well as Sam Adams, was presumably God's work; and if God's will was revealed in his work, how were you to know that the acts of George III, whose nature it was to be tyrannical, were not in accord with Natural Law, while the acts of Sam Adams, whose nature it was to be fond of Liberty, were in accord with Natural Law? Everything in the physical world was certainly part of God's universe, and therefore according to nature; why was not everything in the world of human

relations part of God's universe also, and equally
according to nature?

It was easy enough to read the Book of Nature
in this sense, and even to make verse out of it,
as Pope did.

> All are but parts of one stupendous whole,
>
> Whose body Nature is, and God the soul; . . .
>
> All Nature is but art, unknown to thee;
>
> All chance, direction, which thou canst not see;
>
> All discord, harmony not understood;
>
> All partial evil, universal good:
>
> And, spite of pride, in erring reason's spite,
>
> One truth is clear, whatever is, is right.

According to this reading it seemed that Nature,
having devoured God, was on the point of in-
continently swallowing Man also — a monstrous
conclusion for those who were convinced that
all was *not* right.   That all was not right was a
belief that became widespread and profoundly
held in the latter eighteenth century; and those
who were thus 'steadily intending their minds'
away from the actual political and social order
in search of a better, had at all hazards to make
out that certain aspects of actual human relations were not in harmony with Nature,
while other aspects were.   Convinced that the

torture of Calas, for example, or the Stamp Act, or George III, was something less than 'harmony not understood,' they had to demonstrate that 'life, liberty, and the pursuit of happiness' were according to Nature and the will of God, whereas tyranny and cruelty and the taking of property without consent were not.

This is only another way of saying that in order to find a fulcrum in Nature for moving the existing order, the eighteenth century had to fall back upon the commonplace distinction between good and bad; unless the will of God, as revealed in the nature of man, was to be thought of as morally indifferent, some part of this nature of man had to be thought of as good and some part as bad. The eighteenth century had to appeal, as it were, from nature drunk to nature sober. Now the test or standard by which this appeal could be validly made was found in nature itself — in reason and conscience; for reason and conscience were parts of man's nature too, and God had manifestly given man reason and conscience, as natural guides, precisely in order that he might distinguish that part of his own thought and conduct which was naturally good from that which was naturally bad. Natural law, as a basis for good government, could never be found in the undifferentiated nature of man, but only in human reason applying the test of good and bad to human conduct. Thus the eighteenth century, having apparently ventured so far afield, is nevertheless to be found within hailing distance of the thirteenth; for its conception of natural law in the world of human relations was essentially identical, as Thomas Aquinas' conception had been, with right reason.

It is true that right reason had a much freer field in the eighteenth century than in the thirteenth; it was not limited either by a special revelation or by an established Church; and above all it could appeal for support to history, to the experience of mankind. From the record of human activities in all times and in all places, as well as from the established laws of the material universe, it would be easily possible to verify and to substantiate the verdict of right reason. Whatever the Bible might say, right reason could reject miracles because they were contrary to common sense and the observed procedure of the physical world. Whatever the Church might command, right reason could denounce cruelty and intolerance because the common conscience of mankind revolted at cruelty and intolerance. Whatever the dogmas of particular religions might be, right reason could prefer the precepts of natural Religion which were to be found as Voltaire

said, in the "principles of morality common to
the human race." Whatever customs and positive laws might prevail in particular states,
right reason could estimate their value in the
light of the customs and laws common to all
states. What I have searched for, said Mon-
taigne, is "la connaissance de l'homme en
général" — the knowledge of man in general.[1]
This is precisely what the eighteenth century
did: with the lantern of enlightenment it went
up and down the field of human history looking
for man in general, the universal man, man
stripped of the accidents of time and place;
it wished immensely to meet Humanity and to
become intimate with the Human Race. If it
could find Humanity it would have found man
in general, the natural man; and so it would
have some chance of knowing what were the
rights and laws which, being suited to man in
general, were most likely to be suited to particular men, everywhere and always.

We have now got a long way from the Declaration of Independence and Thomas Jefferson,
and even from John Locke, in whose book
Jefferson found so well expressed the ideas
which he put into the Declaration. Let us
then return to John Locke, whom we have too
long left to his own devices, seeking a 'modi-

---

[1] Quoted in Faguet, *XVIme siècle*, 371.

fied form of the original compact,' being unable to make use of the older version. The older version, which was a compact between the people and God in person, Locke could not use because, as we saw, nature had stepped in between God and man. Locke, like every one else, had therefore to make his way, guided by reason and conscience, through Nature to find the will of God; and the only version of the original compact from which he could derive governmental authority, was such a compact as men, acting according to their nature, would enter into among themselves. Since the will of God was revealed in Nature, you could find out what God had willed governments to be and do only by consulting Nature — the nature of man. ⟨The question which Locke had to answer was therefore this: What kind of political compact would men enter into, if they acted according to the nature which God had given them?⟩

To answer this question, Locke says, we must consider

What state all men are naturally in, and that is, a state of perfect freedom to order their actions and dispose of their possessions and persons, as they think fit, within the bounds of the law of nature, without asking leave, or depending upon the leave of any other man. A state also of equality, wherein all power and jurisdiction is reciprocal, no one having more than another.[1]

This state which all men are 'naturally in,' this state of nature, is not a state of licence; it is a state of perfect freedom and equality, but of freedom and equality only *'within the bounds of the law of nature.'* What is this law of nature?

The state of nature has a law to govern it, which obliges every one: and *reason, which is that law,* teaches all mankind, who will but consult it, that being all equal and independent, no one ought to harm another in his life, health, liberty, or possessions. . . .

In transgressing the law of nature, the offender declares himself to live by another rule than that of *reason and common equity, which is that measure God has set to the actions of men. . . .*

A criminal, who having renounced *reason, the common rule and measure God hath given to mankind,* hath, by the unjust violence and slaughter he hath committed no one, declared war against all mankind.[2]

In Locke's state of nature all men are thus free and all are bound. Is not this a paradox?

---

[1] "Of Civil Government," Bk. II, sec. 4; *Works* (ed. 1812).
[2] *Ibid.*, sec. 6, 8, 11.

No, because the state of nature, in which Locke seeks the origin of government, is not the actual pre-social state of history, but an imaginative state rationally constructed. Locke, like the political writers of the eighteenth century, was not concerned to know how governments had come to be what they were; what he wanted to know was whether there was any justification for their being what they were. "Man is born free, and is everywhere in chains," exclaimed Rousseau. "How was this change made? I do not know. What can make it legitimate? I believe I can answer that question."[1] This is the question Locke seeks to answer — what can justify governments in binding men by positive laws? In order to answer it he first asks what law would bind men if government, positive law, and custom were, conceivably, non-existent? His answer is that in that case no law would bind them except the law of reason. Reason would bind them, because reason is the 'common rule and measure God hath given to mankind'; reason would at once bind and make free; it would, as Locke says, *oblige* every one: but it would oblige them precisely in this, that it would teach them that all are perfectly free and equal and that no one 'ought to harm another in his life, health, liberty, or possessions.'

---

[1] *Du contract social, ou principes du droit politique* (ed. 1762), 2.

Locke's natural law is the law of reason, its only compulsion is an intellectual compulsion, the relations which it prescribes such as would exist if men should follow reason alone.

Such a state as this, an ideal state, in which all men follow the law of reason and no compulsion is necessary — such a state never in fact existed. Therefore let us modify this hypothetical state, so as to bring it a little nearer the reality. Suppose a few men in this rational state, refusing to act rationally, violate the law of nature which is reason, by taking away the 'life, health, liberty or possessions of another.' What is to be done about it? In that case, Locke says, "the execution of the law of nature is . . . put into every man's hands, whereby every one has a right to punish the transgressor of the law, . . . but only . . . so far as calm reason and conscience dictate, what is proportionate to his transgression." [1] Any one who should, for example, commit a murder, might, according to the law of reason, be put to death. "Cain was so fully convinced, that every one had a right to slay such a criminal, that after the murder of his brother, he cries out: 'Every one that findeth me, shall slay me.' So plain was it writ in the hearts of mankind." [2] Thus in this new rational Garden

[1] "Of Civil Government," Bk. II, sec. 8.   [2] *Ibid.*, sec. 11.

of Eden every one is the executor of that natural law of reason which God has written in the hearts of men: if a Cain appears now and then, any one may take his life.

Now it may be, let us suppose so at all events, that a good many Cains will appear, so that all the Abels, the great majority who still live by reason, are in danger of their lives, and are at great inconvenience to defend them. And suppose further that all these rational and conscientious Abels, being a great majority, come together saying: Why should we all be forever going up and down to watch where many Cains come to strike? Go to, let us appoint a few to watch for all. The question is, how might these many Abels be supposed to proceed in this business? Would they not say: These few, whom we appoint to watch for us, that we may be safe in our lives, our health, our liberty and our possessions, are to make what rules are necessary for that purpose, but for that purpose only; and we agree in return to abide by those rules, so long as the few whom we appoint to make the rules do effectively, by means of these rules, make us safe in our lives, our liberties, and our possessions. Such is the modified version of the original compact which Locke finds in the state of nature.

Men being, as has been said, all free, equal, and independent, no one can be put out of his estate, and subjected to the political power of another, without his consent. The only way, whereby any one divests himself of his liberty, and puts on the bonds of civil society, is by agreeing with other men to join and unite into a community, for their comfortable, safe, and peaceable living one amongst another, in a secure enjoyment of their properties, and a greater security against any, that are not of it. . . . When any number of men have so consented to make one community or government, they are thereby presently incorporated, and make one body politic, wherein the majority have a right to act and conclude the rest.[1]

This is all very well, in a hypothetical state of nature; but it might be asked, "it is often asked as a mighty objection, 'Where are, or ever were men in such a state of nature?'"[2] Well, they are so, Locke replies in substance, whenever they find themselves in relation without any positive law to bind them; as, for example, rulers of sovereign states in relation to each other, or the "two men on the desert island, mentioned by Garcilasso de la Vega in

---

[1] *Ibid.*, sec. 95.   [2] *Ibid.*, sec. 14.

his history of Peru." These are in a state of
nature "in reference to one another: for truth
and keeping of faith belongs to men as men, and
not to members of society." Men as *men*
(that is to say man in the abstract, Mon-
taigne's 'man in general') are in the state of
nature. Locke's state of nature is not the actual
pre-social state of history, but the logical non-
social state, which he constructs imaginatively,
as a premise from which to deduce the rational
limits of governmental authority. In the actual
pre-social state of history there may well have
been more Cains than Abels; and no doubt
governments have in fact been established by
custom unconsciously and irrationally submitted to, or by force, by conquest, or by the
flagrant usurpation of kings. This is admitted;
but the fact of tyranny is no more a justification of tyranny in the social state, than the
fact of murder is a justification of murder in
the pre-social state. What Locke is seeking is
not the historical origin, but the rational justification, of government.

If, therefore, any one says that men never did
in fact live in a state where conduct was guided
by reason, but that in fact they originally lived
in a state of confusion and anarchy, in a state
of war, and that "therefore God hath certainly
appointed government to restrain the partiality

and violence of men," the answer is that this is no doubt true. But what do you deduce from this truth? Do you say that because God has appointed governments to restrain the violence of men, it follows that God approves of tyrannical governments because tyrannical governments do in fact exist? If you say so, then you say, with Hobbes, that God approves any government which gets itself established because it gets itself established, and in so far as it has power to maintain itself. Well, Locke says, I do not agree with you.

I easily grant, that civil government is the proper remedy for the inconveniences of the state of nature, which must certainly be great where men may be judges in their own case: . . . but I shall desire those who make this objection, to remember, that absolute monarchs are but men; and if government is to be the remedy of those evils, which necessarily follow from men's being judges in their own cases, and the state of nature is therefore not to be endured; I desire to know what kind of government that is, and how much better it is than the state of nature, where one man commanding a multitude, has the liberty to be judge in his own case, and may do to all his subjects whatever he pleases, without the least liberty to any one to question or control those who execute his pleasure?[1]

The sum and substance of Locke's elaborate enquiry into the origin and character of government is this: since reason is the only sure guide which God has given to men, reason is the only foundation of just government; and so I ask, not what authority any government has in fact, but what authority it ought in reason to have; and I answer that it ought to have the authority which reasonable men, living together in a community, considering the rational interests of each and all, might be disposed to submit to willingly; and I say further that unless it is to be assumed that any existing government has of right whatever authority it exercises in fact, then there is no way of determining whether the authority which it exercises in fact is an authority which it exercises of right, except by determining what authority it ought in reason to have. Stripped of its decorative phrases, of its philosophy of 'Nature' and 'Nature's God' and the 'Universal Order,' the question which Locke asked was a simple one: 'I desire to know what kind of government that is . . . where one man . . . may do to all his subjects whatever he pleases, without the least liberty to

[1] *Ibid.*, sec. 13.

any one to question or control those who execute his pleasure?' This, generally speaking,
was what the eighteenth century desired to
know. The answer which it gave to that question seemed self-evident: Such a government
is a bad government; since governments exist
for men, not men for governments, all governments derive their just powers from the consent
of the governed.

If the philosophy of Locke seemed to Jefferson and his compatriots just 'the common sense
of the matter,' it was not because Locke's
argument was so lucid and cogent that it could
be neither misunderstood nor refuted. Locke's
argument is not particularly cogent unless you
accept his assumptions as proved, nor lucid
until you restate it to suit yourself; on the contrary, it is lumbering, involved, obscured by
innumerable and conflicting qualifications — a
dreary devil of an argument staggering from
assumption posited as premise to conclusion
implicit in the assumption. It was Locke's
conclusion that seemed to the colonists sheer
common sense, needing no argument at all.
Locke did not need to convince the colonists
because they were already convinced; and they
were already convinced because they had long
been living under governments which did, in a
rough and ready way, conform to the kind of

government for which Locke furnished a reasoned foundation. The colonists had never in
fact lived under a government where 'one
man . . . may do to all his subjects whatever
he pleases.' They were accustomed to living
under governments which proceeded, year by
year, on a tacitly assumed compact between
rulers and ruled, and which were in fact very
largely dependent upon 'the consent of the
governed.' How should the colonists not accept
a philosophy, however clumsily argued, which
assured them that their own governments, with
which they were well content, were just the
kind that God had designed men by nature to
have!

The general philosophy which lifted this
common sense conclusion to the level of a cosmic law, the colonists therefore accepted, during
the course of the eighteenth century, without
difficulty, almost unconsciously. That human
conduct and institutions should conform to the
will of God was an old story, scarcely to be
questioned by people whose ancestors were
celebrated, in so many instances, for having
left Europe precisely in order to live by God's
law. Living by God's law, as it turned out,
was much the same as living according to
"the strong bent of their spirits." The strong
bent of their spirits, and therefore God's law,

had varied a good deal according to the locality, in respect to religion more especially; but so far as one could judge at this late enlightened date, God had showered his blessings indifferently upon all alike — Anglicans and Puritans, Congregationalists and Presbyterians, Catholics, Baptists, Shakers and Mennonites, New Lights and Old Lights.   Even Quakers, once thought necessary to be hanged as pestilent blasphemers and deniers of God's will, now possessed a rich province in peace and content.   Many chosen peoples had so long followed God's law by relying upon their own wits, without thereby running into destruction, that experience seemed to confirm the assertion that nature was the most reliable revelation of God's will, and human reason the surest interpreter of nature.

The channels through which the philosophy of Nature and Natural Law made its way in the colonies in the eighteenth century were many. A good number of Americans were educated at British universities, where the doctrines of Newton and Locke were commonplaces; while those who were educated at Princeton, Yale, or Harvard could read, if they would, these authors in the original, or become familiar with their ideas through books of exposition.   The complete works of both Locke and Newton were in the Harvard library at least as early as 1773. Locke's works were listed in the Princeton catalogue of 1760. As early as 1755 the Yale library contained Newton's *Principia* and Locke's *Essay;* and before 1776 it contained the works of Locke, Newton, and Descartes, besides two popular expositions of the Newtonian philosophy. The revolutionary leaders do not often refer to the scientific or philosophical writings of either Newton or Locke, although an occasional reference to Locke's *Essay* is to be found; but the political writings of Locke, Sidney, and Milton are frequently mentioned with respect and reverence. Many men might have echoed the sentiment expressed by Jonathan Mayhew in 1766:

Having been initiated, in youth, in the doctrines of civil liberty, as they were taught by such men as Plato, Demosthenes, Cicero and other renowned persons among the ancients; and such as Sidney and Milton, Locke and Hoadley, among the moderns, I liked them; they seemed rational.[1]

And Josiah Quincy expressed the common idea of his compatriots when, in 1774, he wrote into his will these words:

[1] *The Patriot Preachers of the American Revolution*, 39.

I give to my son, when he shall arrive at the age of 15 years, Algernon Sidney's Works, John Locke's Works, Lord Bacon's Works, Gordon's Tacitus, and Cato's Letters.   May the spirit of Liberty rest upon him![1]

For the general reader, the political philosophy of the eighteenth century was expounded from an early date in pamphlet and newspaper by many a Brutus, Cato, or Popliocola.   An important, but less noticed, channel through which the fundamental ideas of that philosophy — God, Nature, Reason — were made familiar to the average man, was the church. ⟨Both in England and America preachers and theologians laid firm hold of the Newtonian conception of the universe as an effective weapon against infidelity.⟩ Dr. Richard Bentley studied Newton in order to preach a 'Confusion of Atheism,' deriving a proof of Divine Providence from the physical construction of the universe as demonstrated by that 'divine theorist,' Sir Isaac Newton.[2] What a powerful support to Revelation (and to Revolution) was that famous argument from design! The sermons of the century are filled with it — proving the existence and

[1] Rosenthal, "Rousseau at Philadelphia"; *Magazine of American History*, XII, 54.

[2] Brewster, D., *Memoirs of Sir Isaac Newton*, I, 340.   Wheewell, *Inductive Sciences*, I, 421.

the goodness of God from the intelligence which the delicately adjusted mechanism of Nature everywhere exhibited.[1]

In 1750 there was published at Boston a book of Twenty Sermons, delivered in the Parish Church at Charleston, South Carolina, by the Reverend Samuel Quincy. In these sermons we find the Nature philosophy fully elaborated.

For a right knowledge of God by the Light of Nature, displays his several amiable Perfections; acquaints us with the Relation he stands in to us, and the Obligations we owe to him. . . . It teaches us that our greatest Interest and Happiness consists in loving and fearing God, and in doing his Will; that to imitate his moral Perfections in our whole Behaviour, is acting up to the Dignity of our Natures, and that he has endowed us with Reason and Understanding (Faculties which the Brutes have not) on purpose to contemplate his Beauty and Glory, and to keep our inferior Appetites in due Subjection to his Laws, written in our Hearts.[2]

In his famous election sermon of 1754, Jonathan Mayhew uses this philosophy, without the

---

[1] For an admirable statement of the argument, see Hume, "Dialogue on Natural Religion"; *Works* (Green ed.), II, 393.

[2] Quincy, *Twenty Sermons*, 59, 60.

formulae, for deriving the authority of government. Government, he says,

is both the ordinance of God, and the ordinance of man: of God, in respect to his original plan, and universal Providence; of man, as it is more immediately the result of human prudence, wisdom and concert.[1]

In later Massachusetts election sermons, from 1768 to 1773, we find both the philosophy and the formulae; the three concepts of God, Nature, and Reason, which Samuel Quincy made the foundation of religion, are there made the foundation of politics and government as well.[2] And so there crept into the mind of the average man this conception of Natural Law to confirm his faith in the majesty of God while destroying his faith in the majesty of Kings.

English writers in the nineteenth century, perhaps somewhat blinded by British prejudice against the French Revolution and all its works, complacently took it for granted that the political philosophy of Nature and

[1] *A Sermon Preached in the Audience of His Excellency William Shirley, Esq., May 29, 1754*, p. 2.
[2] *A Sermon Preached before His Excellency Francis Bernard, May 25, 1768*, By Daniel Shute. Boston, 1768. *A Sermon Preached . . . May 31, 1769*, By Jason Haven. Boston, 1769. *A Sermon . . . May 30, 1770*, By Samuel Cooke. Boston, 1770. *A Sermon . . . May 29, 1771*, By Frederick Tucker. Boston, 1771. *A Sermon . . . May 27, 1772*, By Moses Parsons. Boston, 1772.

natural rights upon which the Revolution was founded, being particularly vicious must be peculiarly French; from which it followed, doubtless as the night the day, that the Americans, having also embraced this philosophy, must have been corrupted by French influence. The truth is that the philosophy of Nature, in its broader aspects and in its particular applications, was thoroughly English. English literature of the seventeenth and eighteenth centuries is steeped in this philosophy. The Americans did not borrow it, they inherited it. The lineage is direct: Jefferson copied Locke and Locke quoted Hooker. In political theory and in political practice the American Revolution drew its inspiration from the parliamentary struggle of the seventeenth century. The philosophy of the Declaration was not taken from the French. It was not even new; but good old English doctrine newly formulated to meet a present emergency. In 1776 it was commonplace doctrine, everywhere to be met with, as Jefferson said, "whether expressed in conversation, in letters, printed essays, or the elementary books of public right." And in sermons also, he might have added. But it may be that Jefferson was not very familiar with sermons.

CHAPTER III

HISTORICAL ANTECEDENTS OF THE DEC-
LARATION: THEORY OF THE BRITISH
EMPIRE

WHEN the controversy with Great Britain
began in 1764, the preconceptions of the Natural Rights philosophy lay quiescent in colonial
minds, ready to be drawn upon in case of need,
but never yet having been called forth in the
service of any concrete issue. With a possible
exception here and there, the colonists had
never even contemplated the idea of independence. They were, on the contrary, proud to be
counted British subjects and citizens within the
empire, the burdens of which, such as they were,
had never rested heavily upon them. Each
colony had its own government, consisting of a
governor, appointed by the Crown in most
cases, and a legislature of which the lower
house was in all cases elected by certain defined
classes of people resident in the colony. Before
1764 the British Parliament had in the main
confined its supervision to the regulation of
colonial trade, so that each colony had long

been accustomed to exercise, in respect to all internal affairs, a pretty full measure of self-government. Laws passed by the colonial legislatures were often vetoed by the governors, or disallowed by the Crown; but the British government had rarely intervened with regulations of a positive sort, and it had never, with some slight and negligible exceptions, laid a tax on the colonies by act of Parliament.

With this situation the colonies were in the main well satisfied; and when they thought of the constitutional relations by which the colonies were connected with the British empire, they thought of them as relations which permitted the colonists, and doubtless would always permit them, to regulate their own affairs in their own way: the immunities which they in fact enjoyed, they thought of as 'rights' which they ought constitutionally to possess. The truth is, however, that the colonists had not given a great deal of thought to these matters. They had thought a good deal about the respective 'rights' of their assemblies as against the 'rights' of their governors; but there had been no great occasion to ask what were the rights of the assemblies as against the rights of Parliament. The Sugar Act suddenly raised this question; and suddenly called upon to define their rights as colonies within the empire, called upon to say what constitutional barriers there were, if any, against an unlimited Parliamentary control of the colonies, they could immediately find at hand no elaborate or very convincing answer. What most men were thinking was doubtless well enough expressed by two men who committed their opinions to writing in this year of 1764 — Stephen Hopkins, afterwards one of the signers of the Declaration of Independence, and Thomas Hutchinson, afterwards a self-exiled Loyalist.

In a pamphlet entitled *The Rights of the Colonies Examined*, Hopkins argued that all colonies, in ancient and modern times, have always enjoyed "as much freedom as the mother state," and it could hardly be supposed, he thought, that the British colonies were an exception to that rule. Until now, at all events, the British Parliament had understood the rights of the colonies in this sense. Why then should the ancient practices be changed?

The parliament, it is confessed, have power to regulate the trade of the whole empire; and hath it not full power, by this means, to draw all the wealth of the colonies into the mother country at pleasure? What motive, after all this, can remain to induce the parliament to abridge the privileges and lessen the rights of

the most loyal and dutiful subjects, — subjects justly
entitled to ample freedom, who have long enjoyed, and
not abused or forfeited, their liberties, who have used
them to their own advantage in dutiful subserviency to
the orders and interests of Great Britain? Why should
the gentle current of tranquility, that has so long run
with peace through all the British states, and flowed
with joy and happiness in all her countries, be at last
obstructed, be turned out of its true course into unusual
and winding channels, by which many of those states
must be ruined, but none of them can possibly be made
more rich or more happy?

Hopkins does not really define the rights of
the colonies; he raises questions about them.
Have we not rights? We have always enjoyed
rights and privileges, why should we not continue to enjoy them? We have been very dutiful.

Thomas Hutchinson, writing to a friend in
England, speaks of the rights claimed by the
colonies a little more precisely, but still in much
the same sense.

The colonists claim a power of making laws, and a privilege of exemption from taxes, unless voted by their
own representatives. . . . Not one tenth part of the people of Great Britain have a voice in the elections to

Parliament; and, therefore, the colonies can have no claim to it; but every man of property in England may have his voice, if he will. Besides, acts of Parliament do not generally affect individuals, and every interest is represented. But the colonies have an interest distinct from the interest of the nation; and shall the Parliament be at once party and judge? . . .

The nation treats her colonies as a father who should sell the services of his sons to reimburse what they had cost him, but without the same reason; for none of the colonies, except Georgia and Halifax, occasioned any charge to the Crown or kingdom in the settlement of them. The people of New England fled for the sake of civil and religious liberty; multitudes flocked to America with this dependence, that their liberties should be safe. They and their posterity have enjoyed them to their content, and therefore have endured with greater cheerfulness all the hardships of settling new countries. No ill use has been made of these privileges; but the domain and wealth of Great Britain have received amazing addition. Surely the services we have rendered the nation have not subjected us to any forfeitures? [1]

[1] Bancroft, G., *History of the United States* (ed. 1852), V, 206–209.

Such were the first, tentative steps in the effort to find a theory that would meet the emergency — a kind of timid groping about in the dark in search of the half-forgotten British Constitution. During the year 1765, as a result of the discussion which was accompanied by the passage and the practical nullification of the Stamp Act, the conception of colonial rights began to take on a more definite form. Forcible resistance to the Stamp Act, which few people anticipated, proved to be singularly easy, because the act could not take effect without the use of stamped papers, and the bundles of stamped papers, when they were once landed, could be easily destroyed without any one in particular being held responsible for their destruction. The colonists therefore found themselves facing a new emergency. They had to find good and sufficient reasons for having ventured to violate, by open and forcible means, an act of Parliament. They had to have a definition of colonial rights which would make the Stamp Act out to be, not merely an inexpedient measure, but an unconstitutional measure, a measure which the British Parliament had no 'right' to pass.

To meet this emergency, the colonists seized upon the well-established tradition that British liberty had originally been won, and had always been maintained, by a stubborn and persistent parliamentary opposition to arbitrary taxation. This opposition, as a matter of sober historical fact, had never been more than intermittently effective until the seventeenth century; but the parliamentary party of that time, in defense of *their* rights, maintained that the parliamentary control of taxation was as old as Magna Carta. And so in the eighteenth century it was commonly accepted as a principle of the British Constitution that no Englishman could be legally taxed except by his own consent, that is, by his representatives in Parliament. This being so, the colonists reasoned, we, being British subjects with all the rights of Englishmen born within the realm, cannot be legally taxed except with our consent; and therefore, we cannot be legally taxed by the British Parliament since we are not represented in it.

Thus stated, the argument was open to attack at two points: it could be affirmed that Parliament had as a matter of fact taxed the colonies in the past without any opposition on their part; and it could be said that the colonies were represented in Parliament in the same sense that Englishmen were. Soame Jenyns, in a pamphlet widely read in England,[1] pointed out that

---

[1] *The Objections to the Taxation of Our American Colonies, Briefly Considered*. London, 1765. *Works of Soame Jenyns*, II, 189.

many English communities, such as Manchester
and Sheffield, were taxed without being privi-
leged to send representatives to Parliament, so
that the colonies were represented as much or
as little as these English communities; either
Manchester is not represented in Parliament, in
which case Parliament can and does tax Englishmen without their consent, or else Boston is
represented in Parliament, in which case she has
no grievance.   In other words, it was held that
relatively few Englishmen had a right to vote
for their representatives in Parliament; that
they were nevertheless 'virtually represented'
by the members of Parliament chosen by those
who had a right to vote; and that accordingly
the people residing in the colonies were also
'virtually represented' in Parliament in the same
way as the non-electors residing in Great Britain.

This argument was most effectively answered
by Daniel Dulany, of Maryland, in a pamphlet
entitled *Considerations on the Propriety of Imposing Taxes in the British Colonies for the
Purpose of Raising a Revenue by Act of Parliament.* The people of the colonies, says
Dulany, are in a very different situation from
the non-electors residing in Great Britain, because in the latter case the interests of

the non-electors, the electors, and the representatives,
are individually the same, to say nothing of the connection

among neighbors, friends, and relations. The security of the non-electors against oppression is that their oppression will fall also upon the electors and the representatives. . . . Further, if the non-electors should not be taxed by the British Parliament, they would not be taxed at all. . . . Under this constitution, then, a double or virtual representation may be reasonably supposed. The electors, who are inseparably connected in their interests with the non-electors, may be justly deemed to be the representatives of the non-electors, at the same time they exercise their personal privilege in their right of election, and the members chosen, therefore, the representatives of both.

The situation of the colonists was manifestly different. If every inhabitant of America possessed the necessary freehold "not one could vote, but upon the supposition of his becoming a resident of Great Britain." Besides, the colonists already pay taxes levied by their own legislatures, and therefore they would not be exempt from taxation if not taxed by the British Parliament, as the non-electors in Great Britain would be. Most important of all,

there is not that intimate and inseparable relation between the electors of Great Britain and the inhabitants of the colonies, which must inevitably involve both in the same taxation. On the contrary, not a single actual elector in England might be immediately affected by a taxation in America. . . . Even acts oppressive and injurious to an extreme degree, might become popular in England, from the promise or expectation that the very measures which depressed the colonies, would give ease to the inhabitants of Great Britain.

Dulany's refutation of the doctrine of 'virtual representation' was complete — almost too complete. The inference from it was, either that the colonies should be permitted to send representatives to the Parliament, or that the Parliament had no right of taxing the colonies in any way whatever. Sending representatives to Parliament was a perfectly possible thing to do; but the colonists commonly rejected this solution, because it was obvious that sending a few representatives to England would serve only to justify parliamentary taxation without doing anything to prevent it. But, on the other hand, could the colonists stand uncompromisingly on the ground that Parliament had no right to tax them in any way whatever? The Sugar Act was a tax. The Parliament had for over a century imposed trade duties. These were in some sense taxes; and at this early date almost. no one was ready to deny that Parliament had the right to impose taxes of this sort. In face of this difficulty, certain writers drew a distinction between 'internal' and 'external' taxes, denying the right of Parliament to lay the former but admitting, by implication at least, its right to impose the latter. This was no doubt a dangerous admission, and many were inclined to avoid the difficulty by ignoring it. That, for example, is substantially what the Stamp Act Congress did in framing its resolutions of protest against the Stamp Act and the Sugar Act. Expressly affirming that the colonists owed the same allegiance to the Crown of Great Britain as subjects residing in England, the Resolutions declared that "no taxes . . . can be constitutionally imposed upon them but by their respective legislatures"; but without explicitly drawing a distinction between 'internal' and 'external' taxes, the wording of the Resolutions is such as to imply that distinction; the Stamp Act is mentioned as "imposing taxes" which have "a manifest tendency to subvert the rights and liberties of the colonies," while the Sugar Act is only vaguely referred to as among "several late acts" which imposed "duties" that "will be extremely burthensome and grievous."[1]

[1] Macdonald, W., *Documentary Source Book of American History,* 137. Almon, *Prior Documents,* 27, 28.

Thus at the time of the repeal of the Stamp Act in 1766, the colonies did not deny that the British Parliament possessed of right a general legislative jurisdiction over them; they maintained only that this jurisdiction did not include the right of laying taxes upon them without their consent; and that at least direct internal taxes, such as the Stamp Tax, were not only contrary to custom but were a violation of constitutional rights.

The repeal of the Stamp Act was greeted with general rejoicing and thanksgiving, and was accepted for the most part as an admission by the British government of the validity of the colonial contention. It is true, the Parliament categorically refused to admit, in principle, any such thing; on the contrary, the same day the king signed the Repeal bill he signed also the Declaratory Act, which affirmed that the king and Parliament "had, hath, and of right ought to have, full power and authority to make . . . laws and statutes . . . to bind the colonies and people of America . . . in all cases whatsoever."[1] But the colonists were not, for the moment, over sensitive to the assertion of abstract rights, being well content to have won a practical victory. They felt that the Parliament, having repealed the Stamp Act, would

[1] Macdonald, *op. cit.*, 140. Pickering's *Statutes at Large*, XXVII, 19.

be unlikely to pass a new one, or any similar measure laying direct or internal taxes. And if the Parliament in practice held to their distinction between internal and external taxes, what more could they ask, this being the ground on which they had elected, somewhat uncertainly and apprehensively to be sure, to stand in defense of their rights?

It presently appeared that their rights could not be defended on this ground. In 1767 Parliament passed the Townshend Acts. Townshend himself thought the distinction between 'internal' and 'external' taxes "perfect nonsense"; but since the colonists had made a point of it he thought it wise to humor them by laying only 'external' taxes. Certain duties, to be collected in American ports, were accordingly laid upon the importation of various kinds of glass, lead, paper, and tea.[1] The measure was avowedly a tax measure, and it was estimated that the duties might bring in some £40,000 of revenue if efficiently collected; and that these and other duties might be efficiently collected Customs Commissioners were appointed and sent to Boston. Here was an emergency which the colonists had not anticipated. The Commissioners were as great a nuisance as the Stamp Collectors, and more effective, since they

[1] Macdonald, *op. cit.*, 143. Pickering's *Statutes*, XXVII, 505.

did not resign as the Stamp Collectors had done, under pressure, but called in British troops to support them, and actually collected the customs duties, something relatively unknown before. Under the circumstances, the colonists were disposed to agree with Townshend that the distinction between 'internal' and 'external' taxes was "perfect nonsense." After all, a tax was a tax; and the essence of the whole matter was that Parliament had no constitutional power to "take money out of their pockets," as Pitt said, without their consent, by any kind of tax whatever.

A more skilful dialectic was required to maintain this ground than to maintain the old one. It was a somewhat stubborn fact that Parliament had for more than a hundred years passed laws regulating colonial trade, and for regulating trade had imposed duties, some of which had brought into the Exchequer a certain revenue. The Americans could not well say at this late date that Parliament had no right to lay duties in regulation of trade. Must they then submit to the Townshend duties? Or was it possible to make a clear distinction between duties laid for the regulation of trade and duties laid for bringing in a revenue? John Dickinson, in a series of widely read and very influential essays, entitled *Letters from a Farmer in Penn-*

sylvania to the Inhabitants of the British Colonies, attempted to make this distinction. Arguing at length in the old manner that Parliament had no right to tax the colonies without their consent, he maintained that the sole question in respect to the Townshend duties was whether they were duties laid for revenue or for regulation of trade. A difficulty arose from the fact that any duties laid on trade might be both and were likely to be both. Well, said Dickinson, we must determine this question by the 'intention' of the framers of the law. Did the British Parliament pass the Townshend Act primarily with the 'intention' of raising a revenue, or primarily with the intention of regulating trade? Clearly the former, since the intention of raising a revenue was explicitly avowed in the act itself. Hence the Townshend duties were taxes, and as such unconstitutional.

The Townshend Act presented no difficulty on this score; but Dickinson was aware that his method might be difficult to apply in case, as might well be in the future, Parliament should lay duties on trade with the real intention of raising a revenue while openly professing the intention of regulating trade. How then? "It will be difficult for any person but the makers of the laws to determine which of them are made for regulation of trade, and which for raising a revenue." True enough! Well, in that case, since "names will not change the nature of things," the intention of the makers must be inferred from the nature of the law; and Dickinson hoped, for his part, that his countrymen "would never, to their latest existence, want understanding sufficient to discover the intentions of those who rule over them." To derive the nature of an act from the intention of its framers, and the intention of its framers from the nature of the act, was no doubt what logicians would call reasoning in a circle; but whatever the technical defects of the argument might be, the colonists could, and did, lay firm hold of the general conclusion that Americans have "the same right that all states have, of judging when their privileges are invaded."

Meantime, it appeared that their privileges were being invaded in other, and perhaps even more vital, ways than by parliamentary taxation. In 1768, after the Massachusetts Assembly had sent a circular letter to the other colonial assemblies asking for concerted action in defense of their liberties, the Earl of Hillsborough, speaking in the name of the king, categorically directed the Assembly "to rescind the resolution which gave birth to the circular letter from the Speaker, and to declare their disapprobation of, and dissent to, that rash and hasty proceeding."[1] At an earlier date, Governor Colden of New York had been instructed to suspend the meetings of the Assembly of that province until it should have made provision, according to the terms of the Quartering Act, for the support of British troops stationed there.[2] These were measures of ominous import. Of what value was it to safeguard the right of being taxed exclusively in their own assemblies, if the British government could by administrative order abolish their assemblies? If the British government could abolish colonial assemblies, it could destroy every vestige of colonial self-government. Clearly, therefore, the question which was now coming to include all others was the question of preserving the legislative independence of the colonies.

To meet this emergency, a theory which denied the jurisdiction of the British government in this or that particular matter, such as the taxing power, was inadequate; what was needed was a theory which would define the respective jurisdictions of the British and colonial governments in terms of some general principle. Dickinson had said that the colonies were "as much dependent on Great Britain as one

¹ Macdonald, *op. cit.*, 147. *Massachusetts State Papers*, 134. Almon, *Prior Documents*, 220.
² Macdonald, *op. cit.*, 141. Pickering's *Statutes*, XXVII, 609.

free people could be on another." This might
seem to be as indefinite as anything could well
be; but the assumption on which it rests was
to be the foundation upon which the colonists
built up their theory from this time on. That
assumption was that the Americans were one
'people,' the English another, and each a
'free' people. No doubt an Englishman might
have said that this was begging the question;
the precise question at issue, he might have
maintained, is whether the Americans *are* a
'free' people. We maintain that they are subject to the British Parliament. The Parliament
has always exercised jurisdiction over them in
fact; and to prove this we point you to any
number of statutes duly passed and recorded
and submitted to. If positive law is any test,
the colonies are not a 'free' people, but a subject
people; and any privileges which they may have
are privileges granted or permitted by the
British Parliament.

On this ground it was indeed difficult to meet
the British contention. In order to maintain
the rights of a free people, the colonists were
accordingly forced to change the question; and
from this time on we find them less disposed to
ask, What are the rights which we possess as
British subjects? and more disposed to ask,
What are the rights which we possess as mem-

bers of the human race? This latter question was one which Samuel Adams had been thinking about since the year 1743 when, upon receiving the degree of Master of Arts from Harvard College, he argued the thesis, "Whether it be lawful to resist the Supreme Magistrate if the Commonwealth cannot otherwise be preserved." In the present crisis, therefore, he was able to formulate a theory (best stated in a letter to Dennys De Berdt, January 12, 1769) designed to show that the colonies were 'subordinate' but not 'subject' to the British Parliament.[1] Adams' theory of 'subordination' may be taken as the first reasoned elaboration of Dickinson's general proposition that America is "as dependent on Great Britain as one free people can be on another."

For a major premise, Samuel Adams turned as a matter of course to the current philosophy of Natural Rights, familiar doctrine to him, and often enough expounded in newspaper articles or at the Caucus Club; and in bringing it in to solve a practical issue, he doubtless felt that he was only grounding the discussion upon commonly accepted axioms of political thinking. The delimitation of colonial and parliamentary jurisdictions, Adams achieved by subordinating all legislative authority to an authority higher

[1] *Writings of Samuel Adams* (ed. 1904), I, 134.

than any positive law, an authority which no legislature could "overleap without destroying its own foundation." This higher authority was the British Constitution. The British Constitution, Adams said, "is fixed," having its foundation in "the law of God and nature." In the British empire there are many legislatures, all deriving their authority from, and finding their limitations in, the Constitution. Parliament has certainly a supreme or superintending legislative authority in the empire, as the colonial assemblies have a 'subordinate' in the sense of a local, legislative authority; but neither the Parliament nor any colonial assembly can rightly extend its jurisdiction beyond the limits fixed by the Constitution. And therefore, since the Constitution is founded "in the law of God and nature," and since it is "an essential natural right that a man shall quietly enjoy and have the sole disposal of his property," the Americans must enjoy this right equally with Englishmen, and Parliament must be bound to respect this right in the colonies as well as in England; from which it followed that the consent of the colonies must be sought exclusively in their own assemblies, it being manifestly impossible for that consent to be "constitutionally had in Parliament."

Obviously, according to this reasoning, the

authority of the British Parliament over the colonies would ultimately always have to stop where the "essential natural rights" of the colonies began. Adams had found at least one of these rights — the right which every man had of "quietly enjoying and having the sole disposal of his property." But perhaps there were other essential natural rights. What were they? Was there any sure way of finding out? Above all, in case there should be, as might well happen, between Britons and Americans any serious difference of opinion on this point, which opinion should prevail? Admitting that the British Parliament had a supreme or supervising jurisdiction in the empire, it might well be argued that in case of conflict the 'supreme' rather than the 'subordinate' jurisdiction should decide. Some authority would have to determine, in concrete cases, what were and what were not essential natural rights. If this authority were the British Parliament, the essential natural rights were likely to be few indeed; while if the colonial assemblies were to have this authority, the list of essential natural rights was likely in the end to be a long one.

Few men could go more directly to the heart of a question, once he gave his mind to it, than that shrewd old friend of the Human Race, Dr. Benjamin Franklin. Since 1764 he had been giving his mind more or less continuously to this question of colonial rights, and, without making much noise about it, had advanced farther than most men along the road that led to independence. In 1765 it did not appear to him that the Stamp Act was a measure beyond the constitutional jurisdiction of the British Parliament. An inexpedient measure it was certainly, highly burdensome to the colonies, and prejudicial to the true interests of Great Britain; but the only advice Franklin could give his countrymen at that time was to submit to the law as a legally valid act, while protesting against it as in effect an unwise one.

In the meantime Franklin had been reading and reflecting upon all that had been written, pro and con, about the respective rights and prerogatives of British and colonial legislatures. Among other things, he had read and reflected upon the writings of John Dickinson and Samuel Adams. The reasoning of these men seemed to him ingenious and interesting, but not altogether free from over refinement, a quality which was likely to prove a defect in the handling of practical questions. In the year 1768 he formulated the result of his reflections on the whole matter thus:

I am not yet master of the idea these . . . writers have
of the relation between Britain and her colonies. I know

not what the Boston people mean by the "subordination" they acknowledge in their Assembly to Parliament, while they deny its power to make laws for them, nor what bounds the Farmer sets to the power he acknowledges in parliament to "regulate the trade of the colonies," it being difficult to draw lines between duties for regulation and those for revenue; and, if the Parliament is to be the judge, it seems to me that establishing such a principle of distinction will amount to little. The more I have thought and read on the subject, the more I find myself confirmed in opinion, that no middle ground can be well maintained, I mean not clearly with intelligible arguments. Something might be made of either of the extremes: that Parliament has a power to make *all laws* for us, or that it has a power to make *no laws* for us; and I think the arguments for the latter more numerous and weighty, than those for the former. Supposing that doctrine established, the colonies would then be so many separate states, only subject to the same king, as England and Scotland were before the union.[1]

Here at last was a clear-cut alternative — that Parliament had a power of making all laws

[1] *Writings of Benjamin Franklin* (Smyth ed.), V, 115.

for the colonies, or else that it had a power of
making no laws for them. Which should it
be? If it must be one or the other, the arguments
for the latter contention would naturally seem
to the colonists to be more numerous and weighty
than for the former. From this time on Franklin at least assumed that the empire was composed of separate states all subject to the king,
but each possessed of its own legislature outside the jurisdiction of the British Parliament.
By 1770, Franklin felt that this was a position
which should be taken for granted, and no
longer argued.

That the colonies originally were constituted distinct
States, and intended to be continued such, is clear to me
from a thorough consideration of their original Charters,
and the whole conduct of the Crown and nation towards
them until the Restoration. Since that period, the Parliament here has usurped an authority of making laws for
them, which before it had not. We have for some time
submitted to that usurpation, partly through ignorance
and inattention, and partly from our weakness and in-
ability to contend: I hope, when our rights are better
understood here [in Great Britain] we shall, by prudent
and proper conduct, be able to obtain from the equity of

this nation a restoration of them. And in the meantime, I could wish, that such expressions as the supreme authority of Parliament: the subordinancy of our Assemblies to the Parliament, and the like . . . were no more seen in our publick pieces. They are too strong for compliment, and tend to confirm a claim of subjects in one part of the king's dominions to be sovereigns over their fellow subjects in another part of his dominions, when in truth they have no such right, and their claim is founded only in usurpation, the several states having equal rights and liberties, and being only connected, as England and Scotland were before the union, by having one common sovereign, the King.[1]

Franklin's conclusion was better adapted to the purposes of controversy than the methods by which he reached it. His pragmatic mind, instinctively avoiding speculative theory, sought in historical precedent the proof of colonial rights: the Parliamentary legislation for the colonies since 1660 might be regarded as 'usurpation,' because the 'original charters, and the whole conduct of the Crown and nation' demonstrated that the colonies were in origin intended to be independent of Parliamentary

[1] *Ibid.*, 260.

jurisdiction, and were so in fact until the Restoration. For practical purposes, this was perhaps an unstable foundation upon which to rest the whole weight of the colonial contention. The Restoration was after all a long time ago; and the contention that early precedent established the legislative independence of the colonies might be met by the contention that late precedent abolished it. Franklin's conclusion was admirably clean cut, one that the average man could easily grasp; but the argument on which it was founded depended upon nice points in law and history which gave the conclusion at best something less than the force of a self-evident truth. If Franklin's conclusion could be derived from the nature of the universe as well as from the practices of the British empire, it would leave little to be desired as a ground on which to stand in defense of colonial rights.

This fusion of historic and natural rights, which is so perfectly achieved in the Declaration of Independence, was gradually and hesitatingly effected during the years following 1769. James Wilson's pamphlet, *Considerations on the Nature and Extent of the Legislative Authority of the British Parliament*,[1] is perhaps the best example of how the force of circumstances and the exigencies of argument were preparing the

---

[1] *Works of James Wilson* (ed. 1804), III, 199 ff.

minds of the colonists for the general theory which Jefferson was later able to take for granted as the common sense of the matter. Wilson's pamphlet was not published until 1774, but it was written earlier — probably in the year 1770. "The following sheets," the author says, "were written during the late non-importation agreement; but the agreement being dissolved [1770] before they were ready for the press, it was then judged unseasonable to publish them." Wilson, like Franklin, found his ideas of colonial rights expanding with the progress of the controversy; and the process of expounding those rights led him to conclusions which he had not anticipated.

Many will, perhaps, be surprised to see the legislative authority of the British Parliament over the colonies denied in every instance. Those the writer informs, that, when he began this piece, he would probably have been surprised at such opinions himself: for that it was the result, not the occasion, of his disquisitions. He entered upon them with a view and expectation of being able to trace some constitutional line between those cases in which we ought, and those in which we ought not, to acknowledge the power of Parliament over us. In the prosecution of his inquiries, he became fully convinced that such a line does not exist; and that there can be no medium between acknowledging and denying that power in all cases.

Wilson's conclusion is thus the same as Franklin's — that Parliament has no legislative jurisdiction over the colonies; but his argument in support of that conclusion has a wider sweep, the jurisdiction of Parliament being made to depend not merely upon what is "consistent with law," but equally, and indeed fundamentally, upon what is consistent with "the principles of liberty, and with the happiness of the colonies." Those who maintain that the Parliament has power to bind the colonies in all cases, says Wilson, are likely to rest their contention upon the statement of Blackstone, "That there is and must be in every state a supreme, irresistible, absolute, uncontrolled authority, in which the *jus summi imperii*, or the rights of sovereignty, reside"; and they argue, with Blackstone, that in the British Constitution this supreme authority is vested in the king, lords, and commons. This principle, particularly since it was affirmed by Blackstone, no lawyer (and Wilson was a lawyer) could deny. Wilson does not deny it; but he maintains that the importance of the principle "is derived from its tendency to promote the ultimate end of all government"; and accordingly, "if the application of it would, in any instance, destroy, instead of promoting, that end, it ought, in that instance, to be rejected; for to admit it, would be to sacrifice the end to the means, which are valuable only so far as they advance it."

Thus expeditiously does Wilson shift the issue from the positive conception of British sovereignty to the "ultimate end of all government." What then is the ultimate end of all government?

All men are, by nature, equal and free: no one has a right to any authority over another without his consent: all lawful government is founded in the consent of those who are subject to it: such consent was given with a view to ensure and to increase the happiness of the governed, above what they would enjoy in an independent and unconnected state of nature. The consequence is, that the happiness of the society is the first law of every government.

This reminds us of the Declaration of Independence, and sounds as if Wilson were making a summary of Locke. No doubt he was; but it is significant that he keeps as close to his positive law moorings as possible. It is evidently Wilson's aim, or at least it is the effect of his work, so inextricably to unite the positive law applicable to British subjects with the natural law applicable to all men that any apparent conflict between them must necessarily be rejected. If, therefore, any one is disposed to say that Mr. Wilson's assertions about the law of nature are not to be taken seriously as against the eminent Blackstone's affirmation that a "supreme, irresistible, absolute, uncontrolled" authority is vested in the king, lords, and commons, Mr. Wilson immediately stops his mouth by another quotation from the eminent Blackstone: "the law of nature is superior in obligation to any other." Do you quote your Blackstone in support of the sovereignty of the British Parliament? Well, I accept him, as who does not; but I in turn quote him in support of the superior sovereignty of the law of nature. The inferior sovereignty is obviously limited by the superior; and accordingly the British Parliament must be limited by the law of nature, which affirms that the "happiness of the society is the first law of every government."

What has to be asked, therefore, in any discussion of colonial rights, is this:

Will it ensure and increase the happiness of the American colonies, that the British Parliament should possess a supreme, irresistible, uncontrolled authority over them? Is such an authority consistent with their liberty? Have they any security that it will be employed for their good? Such a security is absolutely necessary. Parliaments are not infallible: they are not always just. The members, of whom they are composed, are human; and, therefore, they may err; they are influenced by interest; and, therefore, they may deviate from their duty. . . . It is no breach of decency to suppose all this: the British Constitution supposes it: 'it supposes that parliaments may betray their trust, and provides, as far as human wisdom can provide, that they may not be able to do so long, without a sufficient control.'

Thus the power of sovereignty, being limited by the superior law of nature, which affirms that the happiness of the governed is the ultimate end of all government, must be subject to control by the governed in order that that ultimate end may be attained. How then is this control exercised in the British Constitution?

From this point on Mr. Wilson has only to tread the familiar path of history and positive law. Once more we follow through the old argument that Englishmen are virtually and actually represented in Parliament, while Americans are not represented there in any sense. The Parliament accordingly exercises its 'supreme, irresistible, absolute, uncontrolled' sover-

eign power over Englishmen with their consent;
and is therefore supreme, absolute, uncontrolled only in the immediate action, only so to
speak in determining the present direction of
its power, being controlled ultimately by the
British electorate which may, at a subsequent
election, give another direction to the irresistible power of Parliament by requiring it to
annul its former action. The Americans have
not this power of ultimate control; and if the
Parliament had a legislative power over them
its sovereignty would not only be absolute in
respect to the immediate action, but in respect
to any future action; which is only to say that
its power over them would be arbitrary and des-
potic, something contrary to the spirit of British
history and the genius of the British Constitution. In further support of this familiar argument, Wilson digs up numerous cases out of
"the books of the law," going back to the time
of Richard III, to that famous Calvin's case
(properly cited, as became a lawyer — *4.
Mod. 225. 7. Rep. 22.*) in which the highest
British court had decided that the Irish were
not bound by British statutes "because they do
not send knights to Parliament." In the reigns
of William and Mary similar decisions had been
made in respect to Jamaica and Virginia.

Thus Mr. Wilson proved that natural law,

the British Constitution, and the decisions of
British courts with one voice proclaimed the
colonies outside the jurisdiction of Parliament;
from which it followed that the colonies must be
subject only to the jurisdiction of their own
legislatures. If it should be objected that this
was to renounce "all dependence on Great
Britain," his reply was no, the colonies are
dependent on Great Britain in the sense that
they owe "obedience and loyalty . . . to the
kings of Great Britain." The connection between the inhabitants of Great Britain and
those of America is the connection of fellow
subjects:

They are under allegiance to the same prince; and this

union of allegiance naturally produces a union of hearts.

It is also productive of a union of measures through the

whole British dominions. To the king is intrusted the

direction and management of the great machine of gov-

ernment. . . . He makes war: he concludes peace: he

forms alliances: he regulates domestic trade by his pre-

rogative, and directs foreign commerce by his treaties

with those nations, with whom it is carried on. He

names the officers of government; so that he can check

every jarring movement in the administration. He has

a negative on the different legislatures throughout his

dominions, so that he can prevent any repugnancy in their different laws. The connexion and harmony between Great Britain and us, which it is her interest and ours mutually to cultivate, and on which her prosperity, as well as ours, so materially depends, will be better preserved by the operation of the legal prerogatives of the crown, than by the exertion of an unlimited authority by Parliament.

Mr. Wilson's theory of the relations of the colonies to Great Britain was essentially the same as that which we find in the Declaration of Independence. Meanwhile, during the years from 1770 to 1774, the manuscript in which these views were expressed lay unread in its author's desk. Wilson may have supposed, as many men did, that the controversy with Great Britain was at last happily in the way of being composed. But in the year 1773, when the British Parliament conferred upon the East India Company privileges which gave to that British corporation a virtual monopoly of the American tea trade, the old dispute flared up in a more embittered form. December 16, 1773, the cargo of tea which the East India Company sent to Boston was dumped into the harbor by the Boston patriots. To this act of violence, Parliament replied by passing with overwhelming majorities the Coercive Acts:[1] remodelling the Massachusetts Charter; authorizing the transfer to English courts of cases involving either a breach of the peace or the conduct of officials in the performance of their duties; providing for the quartering of British troops upon the inhabitants; and closing the port of Boston until that town should have made reparation for the destroyed tea. To give these measures effect, General Gage, the commander of the military forces in America, was made governor of Massachusetts. "The die is now cast," the king wrote to Lord North; "the colonies must either submit or triumph."

The colonies were not disposed to submit; but they realized that a crisis had arrived, and in order to meet it effectively a congress of deputies from all the colonies was called to meet in Philadelphia. When the Congress assembled, September 5, 1774, every one thought that something ought to be done, and that that something, whatever it might be, ought to be supported by every colony, and by every man who wished to be thought an American patriot. But as to what that something was that ought to be done, there was naturally a great diversity of opinion. The general feeling was that if the colonies could convince the British people

[1] Pickering's *Statutes*, XXX, 336, 367, 381.

that they were in dead earnest about their rights, and without wishing for independence were thoroughly united in the determination to defend them, the British government would back down in this case as it had done before. Congress was not an association of scholars assembled to conduct a scientific investigation into the legal and historical basis of the British Constitution, but a political body endeavoring to bring about a certain practical result. This primary practical aim was to unite the colonies on measures which would be most likely to induce the British government to make concessions. Inevitably, therefore, the resulting action of Congress, both as to what it did and as to what it said, was a compromise. Its Declaration of Rights was necessarily such a compromise. The Congress, in framing its declaration, was in the nature of the case less concerned with the logical coherence and validity of the statement which it made, than with making such a statement as would be acceptable to the greatest number of Americans, and at the same time best adapted to win concessions from Great Britain.

If, therefore, the first Continental Congress did not adopt the theory of British-American relations which we find in the Declaration of Independence, it was not because the theory was a novel one. In 1774 it was familiar doctrine to all men; and the most radical were quite ready to take their stand upon it at that time. Before departing for the Virginia Convention Jefferson prepared, as he says, "what I thought might be given, as instruction, to the Delegates who should be appointed to attend the general congress." This paper, afterwards printed as *A Summary View of the Rights of British America*,[1] does not formulate or argue the theory that the colonies are bound to Great Britain only through the king; it takes it for granted; the theory is implicit in the statement, as it is in the Declaration of Independence. Jefferson would address the remonstrance to the king, who should be "reminded"

that our ancestors, before they emigrated to America, were the free inhabitants of the British dominions in Europe, and possessed a right which nature has given all men, of departing from the country in which chance, not choice, has placed them, of going in quest of new habitations, and of there establishing new societies, under such laws and regulations as to them shall seem most likely to promote public happiness. . . . That settlement having been made in the wilds of America, the

[1] *Writings of Thomas Jefferson* (Ford ed.), I, 421 ff.

emigrants thought proper to adopt that system of laws under which they had hitherto lived in the mother country, and to continue their union with her by submitting themselves to the same common Sovereign, who was thereby made the central link connecting the several parts of the Empire thus newly multiplied.

Unhappily the British Parliament, from an early date, usurped a power of legislating for the colonies; among other things, restricting "the exercise of a free trade with all parts of the world, possessed by the American colonists, as of natural right"; and these unjust encroachments, once established, were followed by others, which in late years had so multiplied as no longer to be tolerable. Having thus by implication set forth the theory of the constitution of the empire, Jefferson goes on to specify the several acts of the British Parliament which are obviously, from the point of view of this theory, unconstitutional.

Jefferson, falling ill on the way to the Convention, forwarded two copies of his paper, one of which was laid before the assembly by Peyton Randolph. But "tamer sentiments were preferred," Jefferson says, "and, I believe, wisely preferred; the leap I proposed being too long, as yet, for the mass of our citizens." Of the reception of Jefferson's paper in the Virginia Convention, Edmund Randolph says, in his MSS History of Virginia:

He forwarded by express for the consideration of its members a series of resolutions. I distinctly recollect the applause bestowed on the most of them, when they were read to a large company at the house of Peyton Randolph, to whom they were addressed. Of all the approbation was not equal. From the celebrated letters of the Pennsylvania Farmer we had been instructed to bow to the external taxation of Parliament [This was not quite just to the Farmer] as resulting from our migration, and a necessary dependence on the mother country. But this composition of Mr. Jefferson shook this conceded principle although it had been confirmed by a still more celebrated pamphlet of Daniel Dulaney of Maryland, and cited by Lord Chatham as a text book of American rights. [Dulany, not Dickinson, was cited by Chatham.] The young ascended with Mr. Jefferson to the source of those rights, the old required time for consideration before they could tread this lofty ground, which, if it had not been abandoned, at least had not been fully occupied throughout America.

If the first Continental Congress did not, in respect to the theory of American rights, occupy the lofty ground of Mr. Jefferson, neither did it take the lower ground of Mr. Dickinson; it seems, on the contrary, to have stood midway between these two positions, inviting every man to take which of them he found most comfortable. What the difficulties were that led Congress to take this stand we learn in part from that invaluable *Diary* of John Adams, who was a member of the committee appointed to prepare the Declaration of Rights. In some brief notes of the debates in the committee[1] Adams gives us an illuminating glimpse of the conflicting opinions that had to be reconciled; and in his *Autobiography*, written in 1805, we find the following statement of the way in which that conflict worked itself out to a practical conclusion.

It would be endless to attempt even an abridgment of the discussions in this committee, which met regularly every morning for many days successively. . . . The two points which labored the most were: 1. Whether we should recur to the law of nature, as well as to the British Constitution, and our American charters and grants. Mr. Galloway and Mr. Duane were for excluding the

[1] *Works of John Adams*, II, 370.

law of nature. I was very strenuous for retaining and insisting on it, as a resource to which we might be driven by Parliament much sooner than we were aware. 2. The other great question was, what authority we should concede to Parliament; whether we should deny the authority of Parliament in all cases; whether we should allow any authority to it in our internal affairs; or whether we should allow it to regulate the trade of the empire with or without any restrictions. . . . After several days deliberation, we agreed upon all the articles excepting one, and that was the authority of Parliament, which was indeed the essence of the whole controversy; some were for a flat denial of all authority; others for denying the power of taxation only; some for denying internal, but admitting external, taxation. After a multitude of motions had been made, discussed, negatived, it seemed as if we should never agree upon anything. Mr. John Rutledge of South Carolina, one of the Committee, addressing himself to me, was pleased to say, "Adams, we must agree upon something; you appear to be as familiar with the subject as any one of us, and I like your expressions, — 'the necessity of the case,' and 'excluding all ideas of taxation, external and internal'; I have a great opinion of that same idea of the necessity of the case, and I am determined against all taxation for revenue. Come, take the pen and see if you can't produce something that will unite us." Some others of the committee seconding Mr. Rutledge, I took a sheet of paper and drew up an article. When it was read, I believe not one of the committee was fully satisfied with it; but they all soon acknowledged that there was no hope of hitting on anything in which we could all agree with more satisfaction. All therefore agreed to this, and upon this depended the union of the Colonies.[1]

In the light of this illuminating passage (quite possibly inaccurate in some details, having been written in 1805), we can understand the Declaration of Rights adopted by the first Congress. We can understand why the resolutions avoided theory as much as possible; why they 'declared' more than they argued or expounded, confining themselves in the main to stating the specific rights which the colonies claimed; why in certain cases this statement is ambiguous, being couched in phrases that could be taken to mean more or less, according to the disposition of the reader. The Declaration states, to begin with,

[1] *Ibid.*, 373, 374.

That the inhabitants of the English colonies in North America, by the immutable laws of nature, the principles of the English Constitution, and the several charters or compacts, have the following RIGHTS:

Every reader could take his choice, according to disposition laying most stress on the natural law, or on the principles of the British Constitution as he understood those principles, or else on the colonial charters, documents which he might indeed prefer to call *compacts*. Having laid this broad foundation for the rights of the colonies, the Declaration goes on to declare what these rights specifically are.

That they are entitled to life, liberty and property; and they have never ceded to any foreign power whatever [to France, for example. To the British Parliament? Well, you may include it among foreign powers if you like.] a right to dispose of either without their consent.

That our ancestors, who first settled these colonies, were at the time of their emigration from the mother country, entitled to all the rights, liberties, and immunities of free and natural-born subjects, within the realm, of England.

That by such emigration they by no means forfeited, surrendered, or lost any of those rights, but that they were, and their descendants now are, entitled to the exercise of all such of them, as their local and other circumstances enable them to exercise and enjoy.

That the foundation of English liberty, and of all free government, is a right in the people to participate in their legislative council: and as the English colonists are not represented, and from their local and other circumstances, cannot properly be represented in the British Parliament, they are entitled to a free and exclusive power of legislation in their several provincial legislatures, where their right of representation can alone be preserved, in all cases of taxation and internal polity, subject only to the negative of their sovereign, in such manner as has been heretofore used and accustomed:

Thus far resolution number four; very carefully stated, with all possible qualification; probably satisfactory as it stands to Mr. Dickinson and many men; but not satisfactory to Mr. Adams and many others, who do not wish to admit the legislative authority of the British Parliament in all cases of *external* polity, or to give to it an unlimited power of regulating colonial trade. What shall be done about this knotty point? The rest of resolution four must be the phrasing by which Mr. Adams was at last able to satisfy every one in part by satisfying no one fully; a phrasing which admits the authority of Parliament as of fact, which does not expressly deny it as of right, but which by implication leaves it to be supposed that the exercise of that authority both as of fact and of right is dependent upon the consent of the colonies, which at present they give but may in future withdraw.

But, from the necessity of the case, and a regard to the mutual interest of both countries, *we cheerfully consent* to the operation of such acts of the British Parliament, as are *bona fide* restrained to the regulation of our external commerce, for the purpose of securing the commercial advantages of the whole empire to the mother country, and the commercial benefits of its respective members; excluding every idea of taxation internal or external, for raising a revenue on the subjects, in America, without their consent.[1]

Rough sledding this; but once over the difficult ground, all is smooth enough going the rest of the way.

[1] Macdonald, *op. cit.*, 162. *Journals of Congress* (Ford ed.), I, 63.

Both the objects and the methods of the first Congress were those also of the second Congress until the year 1776.   In the spring and summer of 1775, even after the Battle of Lexington had precipitated a state of war, the belief still persisted that Great Britain would in the end back down if the colonies only remained united and made it clear that even now they desired reconciliation and not independence.   It was still necessary therefore to satisfy the timid as well as the aggressive.   The timid wished to rely primarily upon petition and remonstrance and the non-intercourse measures.   One day Mr. Dickinson, following John Adams out of the Congress hall, said to him in great heat: "What is the reason, Mr. Adams, that you New England men oppose our measures of reconciliation? There now is Sullivan, in a long harangue, following you in a determined opposition to our petition to the king.   Look ye!   If you don't concur with us in our pacific system, I and a number of us will break off from you in New England, and we will carry on the opposition by ourselves in our own way."   Mr. Adams was at that moment "in a very happy temper," which was not always the case, and so, he says, he was able to reply very coolly.   "Mr. Dickinson, there are many things which I can very cheerfully sacrifice to harmony, and even to unanimity; but I am not to be threatened into an express adoption or approbation of measures which my judgment reprobates. Congress must judge, and if they pronounce against me, I must submit, as, if they determine against you, you ought to acquiesce." [1]

Congress did decide. It decided to adopt Mr. Dickinson's petition; and to this measure Mr. Adams submitted, not without confiding to James Warren his opinion that "a certain great Fortune and piddling Genius . . . has given a silly Cast to our whole Doings." [2] But the Congress also decided to raise a continental army for carrying on armed resistance; appointed George Washington, Esq. Commander in Chief of that army; and in justification of these measures published a Declaration of the Causes and Necessity of Taking up Arms.

This Declaration, taking no account of Mr. Dickinson's opposition to Mr. Adams' measures or of Mr. Adams' opposition to Mr. Dickinson's measures, affirmed that "our union is perfect." It also proclaimed the object of this perfect union.

We have not raised armies with ambitious designs of separating from Great Britain. . . . We shall lay them

---

[1] *Works of John Adams*, II, 410.
[2] *Warren-Adams Letters*, I, 88.

down when hostilities shall cease on the part of the aggressors. . . . With an humble confidence in the mercies of the supreme and impartial Judge and Ruler of the Universe, we . . . implore his divine goodness to protect us through this great conflict, to dispose our adversaries to reconciliation on reasonable terms, and therefore to relieve the empire of the calamities of civil war.[1]

The hope of reconciliation died slowly. Even after the king refused to receive the Petition, even after the British Government issued the Prohibitory Act, December 22, 1775, which declared the colonies out of its protection and proclaimed a blockade of all their ports, many men still clung to this hope. They clung to it in desperation, partly because they had so often and so explicitly declared that separation was no part of their purpose and utterly abhorrent to their desire. But besides all this, most Americans did in fact look forward with apprehension to a permanent disruption of the British empire. They had long been proud of the British empire, of its achievements, of its name and fame in the world; it was their empire too; they bore the name and shared the fame. What Americans clung to with desperation, and

[1] Macdonald, *op. cit.*, 177. Preliminary drafts of the Declaration on Taking up Arms by Jefferson and Dickinson, as well as the final draft, are in *Journals of Congress* (Ford ed.), II, 128, 140.

relinquished with regret, was that traditional but now vanishing conception of themselves as a people sharing the rich inheritance of English history and freely contributing to its enlargement and perpetuation. To surrender this conception was to renounce the prepossessions that had given consistence to all their thought, to suppress the emotions that had sustained and fortified their lives.

Not desire, but practical difficulties, forced them to adopt separation from Great Britain as the object of their efforts. In the winter of 1776 the trend of opinion was towards independence as the only alternative to submission. The first Congress had adopted the non-intercourse measure in order to force Great Britain to make concessions; the second Congress had taken up arms in order to force Great Britain to make concessions. If Great Britain made concessions speedily, all would be well; but if she insisted on making war the colonies would have to abandon either the war measure or the non-intercourse measure. As Mr. Zubly kept repeating in Congress, the colonies must speedily obtain one of two things — "A reconciliation with Great Britain or the means of carrying on the war."[1] They could not carry on war with one hand, while destroying the trade and pros-

[1] *Works of John Adams*, II, 469.

perity of the colonies with the other. "We are between hawk and buzzard," said Livingston; "we puzzle ourselves between the warlike and the commercial opposition."[1] To carry on war they must revive trade; to revive trade they must obtain protection for it; to obtain this protection they must have a "treaty with a foreign power." But "in what character shall we treat?" asked Mr. Wythe. "As subjects of Great Britain — as rebels? If we should offer our trade to the Court of France, would they take notice of it any more than if Bristol or Liverpool should offer theirs, while we profess to be subjects? No. We must declare ourselves a free people."[2] Without the aid of France the colonies could not long wage war against Great Britain; and to obtain the aid of France they had to make it plain to her that they were fighting for independence and not reconciliation. From April 6, 1776, when the Congress opened the colonial ports to the trade of the world, the Declaration of Independence was therefore a foregone conclusion. "As to declarations of independency," wrote John Adams, "read our privateering laws and our commercial laws. What signifies a word?"

From this moment the old policy of compromise was rapidly abandoned. Those who on

[1] *Ibid.,* 461.   [2] *Ibid.,* 486.

this ground would not support the patriot cause had to be ignored or suppressed; and now that independence was the object, it was not only possible but necessary, in formulating the rights of the colonies, to adopt a theory of British-colonial relations in the light of which the act of separation could be regarded as a step that the colonies had always had a moral and legal right to take. Such a theory could only be found in a close union of the natural rights philosophy of government with a conception of the empire as a confederation of free peoples submitting themselves to the same king by an original compact voluntarily entered into, and terminable, in the case of any member, at the will of the people concerned. Such is the theory which, suggested by Franklin as early as 1768, elaborated by Wilson in 1770, and taken for granted by Jefferson in 1774, determines the form and character of the Declaration of Independence and gives to it a high degree of organic unity.

In the Declaration the natural rights philosophy, although clearly formulated, is not argued but is taken for granted; the theory of British-colonial relations is not even formulated, but lies as it were embedded in the statement of grievances against the king, a kind of concealed framework upon which Jefferson built up his finished structure of concrete oppressions. Expressly stated, the theory that is implicit in the Declaration might be put somewhat as follows:

We are not subject to Parliament. We are a free people, whose ancestors, in accord with the natural right of all men, emigrated to the wilds of America, and there established at the hazard of their lives and fortunes new societies, with forms of government suitable to their conditions and agreeable to their ideas. We have our own legislatures to govern us, just as our British brethren have their legislature. The British Parliament, which is their legislature, has no authority over us, any more than our legislatures have authority over them. We do not mention the British Parliament in our Declaration of Independence because we are not declaring independence of an authority to which we have never been subject. We are declaring ourselves independent of the king, because it is to the king only that we have ever been subject; and in dissolving our connection with the king we separate from the British empire, because it is only through the king that we have ever had any connection with the British empire. This connection we voluntarily entered into by submitting ourselves to the sovereign head of the empire. Subjects of the king we have professed ourselves to be, and loyal subjects, in the sense that as a free people we acknowledged allegiance to him personally, thereby freely assuming the obligations that go with allegiance. But this allegiance to the king, while it obligates us to support the empire in so far as we can and in the manner we find convenient, gives him no right of compulsion over us. If we separate from the empire, it is because the king has attempted to exert such compulsion, and by repeated acts of usurpation has exhibited a determination to subject us to his arbitrary power. In declaring our independence of the king, and thus separating from the British empire, we are not breaking off a complicated set of intimate relationships, sanctioned by positive law and long established custom; on the contrary, we are only snipping the thin gold thread of voluntary allegiance to a personal sovereign. As a free people we have formerly professed allegiance to the king as the formal head of the empire; as a free people we now renounce that allegiance; and this renunciation we justify, not in virtue of our rights as British subjects, but in virtue of those natural rights which we, in company with all men, are inalienably possessed of.

Thus step by step, from 1764 to 1776, the colonists modified their theory to suit their needs. They were not altogether unaware of the fact. "Shall we," cries a Virginian in despair, "Proteus-like perpetually change our ground, assume every moment some new strange shape, to defend, to evade?" This was precisely what could not be avoided; for the underlying purpose which conditioned their action was always the determination to be free. They felt that they had been free in fact, and that they ought therefore to be free in law. "British subjects," said Franklin in 1755, "by removing to America, cultivating a wilderness, extending the domain, and increasing the wealth, commerce, and power of the mother country, at the hazard of their lives and fortunes, ought not, and in fact do not thereby lose their native rights." Profoundly convinced that they deserved to be free, Americans were primarily concerned with the moral or rational basis of their claims. "To what purpose is it to ring everlasting changes . . . on the cases of Manchester . . . and Sheffield?" exclaims James Otis. "If these now so considerable places are not represented, they ought to be." This "ought to be" is the fundamental premise of the whole colonial argument. But the "ought to be" is not ultimately to be found in positive law and custom, but only in something outside of, beyond, above the positive law and custom. Whenever men become sufficiently dissatisfied with what is, with the existing regime of positive law and custom, they will be found reaching out beyond it for the rational basis of what they conceive ought to be. This is what the Americans did in their controversy with Great Britain; and this rational basis they found in that underlying preconception which shaped the thought of their age — the idea of natural law and natural rights.

CHAPTER IV

DRAFTING THE DECLARATION

THE committee appointed June 11, 1776, to prepare a declaration of independence consisted of Jefferson, Adams, Franklin, Sherman, and Robert R. Livingston. In his *Autobiography*,[1] written in 1805, and again in a letter to Pickering, written in 1822, Adams says that the Committee of Five decided upon "the articles of which the declaration was to consist," and it then appointed Jefferson and himself a sub-committee to "draw them up in form." When the sub-committee met, he says,

Jefferson proposed to me to make the draught, I said I will not; You shall do it. Oh no! Why will you not? You ought to do it. I will not. Why? Reasons enough. What can be your reasons? Reason 1st. You are a Virginian and a Virginian ought to appear at the head of this business. Reason 2nd. I am obnoxious, suspected and unpopular; you are very much otherwise. Reason 3rd. You can write ten times better than I can. 'Well,'

[1] *Ibid.*, 512.

said Jefferson, 'if you are decided I will do as well as I can.' Very well, when you have drawn it up we will have a meeting.[1]

Jefferson's account is different. Writing to Madison in 1823, he says:

Mr. Adams memory has led him into unquestionable error. At the age of 88 and 47 years after the transactions, . . . this is not wonderful. Nor should I . . . venture to oppose my memory to his, were it not supported by written notes, taken by myself at the moment and on the spot. . . . The Committee of 5 met, no such thing ·as a sub-committee was proposed, but they unanimously pressed on myself alone to undertake the draught. I consented; I drew it; but before I reported it to the committee I communicated it separately to Dr. Franklin and Mr. Adams requesting their corrections; . . . and you have seen the original paper now in my hands, with the corrections of Dr. Franklin and Mr. Adams interlined in their own handwriting. Their alterations were two or three only, and merely verbal. I then wrote a fair copy, reported it to the committee, and from them, unaltered to the Congress.[2]

[1] *Ibid.*, 514.
[2] *Writings of Thomas Jefferson* (ed. 1869), VII, 304.

This 'original paper' of which Jefferson speaks, 'with the corrections of Dr. Franklin and Mr. Adams interlined in their own handwriting,' is commonly known as the Rough Draft. It has been preserved, and may now be seen in the Library of Congress in Washington, or, in excellent facsimile, in Mr. Hazelton's indispensable work on the Declaration of Independence.[1] A more interesting paper, for those who are curious about such things, is scarcely to be found in the literature of American history. But the inquiring student, coming to it for the first time, would be astonished, perhaps disappointed, if he expected to find in it nothing more than the 'original paper . . . with the corrections of Dr. Franklin and Mr. Adams interlined in their own handwriting.' He would find, for example, on the first page alone nineteen corrections,

---

[1] *The Declaration of Independence: Its History.* New York. 1906. Whether the Rough Draft which Jefferson refers to in his letter to Madison was the first draft which he made for the Declaration is not known. But it appears that he used, in preparing the Declaration, a manuscript now in the Library of Congress, which is in Jefferson's hand, and is endorsed by him as follows: "Constitution of Virginia first ideas of Th: J. communicated to a member of the Convention." The first page of this manuscript is in the form of a series of reasons why Virginia repudiates her allegiance to George III. The charges against the king which appear in the Rough Draft seem to have been copied, in many cases verbatim, from this manuscript. Cf. Fitzpatrick, J. C. "The Manuscript from which Jefferson Wrote the Declaration of Independence"; in *Daughters of the American Revolution Magazine,* LV, 363.

additions, or erasures besides those in the hand-writing of Adams and Franklin. It would probably seem to him at first sight a bewildering document, with many phrases crossed out, numerous interlineations, and whole paragraphs enclosed in brackets. Can this be the 'original paper' which Jefferson refers to? Can this be the Rough Draft which Jefferson submitted to Franklin and Adams?

Yes and no. Jefferson seemed not to be aware that future students of history would wish to see the 'original paper' just as he wrote it; on the contrary, this precious sheet was to him a rough draft indeed, upon which he could conveniently indicate whatever changes might be made in the process of getting the Declaration through the Committee of Five, and afterward through Congress. The Rough Draft in its present form is thus the 'original paper,' together with all, or nearly all, the corrections, additions, and erasures made between the day on which Jefferson submitted it to Franklin and Adams and the 4 of July when Congress adopted the Declaration in its final form. The inquiring student, if he has the right kind of curiosity, will not after all be disappointed to learn this; on the contrary, he will be delighted at the prospect of reading, in this single document, with some difficulty it is true, the whole history of the drafting of the Declaration of Independence.

In this history there are obviously three stages of importance: the Declaration as originally written by Jefferson; the Declaration as submitted by the Committee of Five to Congress; the Declaration as finally adopted. The Declaration as finally adopted is to be found in the Journals of Congress; but that 'fair copy' which Jefferson speaks of as the report of the Committee of Five has not been preserved;[1] while the original Rough Draft, as we have

---

[1] It is possible that Jefferson was mistaken in thinking that he made a 'fair copy' for the Committee. If he made such a copy, and if it was handed in as the report of the Committee, it seems odd that it was not preserved among the papers of Congress. If there was such a copy, it was undoubtedly that copy as amended by Congress that was used by Dunlap for printing the text that was pasted into the 'rough' Journal; and it is at least conceivable that it was inadvertently left with the printer, and so lost. On the other hand, if there was no 'fair copy,' we must suppose that the corrected Rough Draft was itself the report of the Committee. I find it difficult to suppose that Jefferson would have presented, as the formal report of the Committee, a paper so filled with erasures and interlineations that in certain parts no one but the author could have read it without a reading glass. Besides, if the Rough Draft was handed in as the report of the Committee it should bear the endorsement of the Secretary of Congress, Charles Thompson. No such endorsement appears on the Rough Draft. Again, if the Rough Draft was used as the report of the Committee, one would suppose that the amendments made by Congress would be indicated on it in the hand of Charles Thompson; whereas they are in fact in the hand of Jefferson. On the whole, the reasons for supposing that Jefferson made a 'fair copy,' which was used as the report of the Committee and afterward lost, seem to me more convincing than the reasons for supposing that the Rough Draft itself was used as the report of the Committee.

seen, seems to have been used by Jefferson as a memorandum upon which to note the later changes. How then can we reconstruct the text of the Declaration as it read when Jefferson first submitted it to Franklin and Adams? For example, Jefferson first wrote "we hold these truths to be sacred & undeniable." In the Rough Draft as it now reads, the words "sacred & undeniable" are crossed out, and "self-evident" is written in above the line. Was this correction made by Jefferson in process of composition? Or by the Committee of Five? Or by Congress? There is nothing in the Rough Draft itself to tell us. As it happens, John Adams made a copy of the Declaration which still exists.[1] Comparing this copy with the corrected Rough Draft, we find that it incorporates only a very few of the corrections: one of the two corrections which Adams himself wrote into the Rough Draft; one, or possibly two, of the five corrections which Franklin wrote in; and eight verbal changes apparently in Jefferson's hand. This indicates that Adams must have made his copy from the Rough Draft when it was first submitted to him; and we may assume that the eight verbal changes, if

---

[1] This copy is in the possession of the Massachusetts Historical Society. It is printed in Hazelton, *op. cit.*, 306 ff; in *Journals of Congress* (Ford ed.), V, 491; and in *Writings of Jefferson* (Ford ed.), II, 42. For a brief discussion of the document, see Hazelton, 346.

in Jefferson's hand, which we find incorporated in Adams' copy, were there when Jefferson first submitted the Draft to Adams — that is, they were corrections which Jefferson made in process of composing the Rough Draft in the first instance. With Adams' copy in hand it is therefore possible to reconstruct the Rough Draft as it probably read when first submitted to Franklin.

THE ROUGH DRAFT

(as it probably read when Jefferson first submitted it to Franklin.) [1]

A Declaration by the Representatives of the UNITED STATES OF AMERICA, in General Congress assembled.

When in the course of human events it becomes necessary for a people to advance from that subordination in which they have hitherto remained, & to assume among the powers of the earth the equal & independent

---

[1] The text here given is identical with the Adams copy except, (1) the corrections of Franklin and Adams appearing on the Rough Draft and incorporated by Adams in his copy are omitted, (2) the spelling, capitalization, and punctuation of the Rough Draft have been followed, (3) in a number of instances where Adams obviously made slips in copying, the Rough Draft is followed. These slips, in each case, are indicated in the footnotes.

station to which the laws of nature & of nature's god entitle them, a decent respect to the opinions of mankind requires that they should declare the causes which impel them to the change.

We hold these truths to be ~~sacred and undeniable;~~ self-evident;[1] that all men are created equal & independent; that from that equal creation they derive ~~in~~ rights inherent & inalienable,[2] among which are the preservation of life, & liberty, & the pursuit of happiness; that to secure these ends, governments are instituted among men, deriving their just powers from the consent of the governed; that whenever any form of government shall become destructive of these ends, it is the right of the people to alter or to abolish it, & to institute new government, laying it's foundation on such principles & organizing it's powers in such form, as to them shall seem most likely to effect their safety .& happiness.   prudence indeed will dictate that governments long established

---

[1] It is not clear that this change was made by Jefferson.   The handwriting of "self-evident" resembles Franklin's.

[2] Adams' copy reads "unalienable."   This is the reading of the Declaration as finally adopted; but as the change is not indicated on the Rough Draft, Adams must have deliberately or inadvertently made the change in copying.   See below, p. 175, note 1.

should not be changed for light & transient causes:[1]
and accordingly all experience hath shewn that mankind
are more disposed to suffer while evils are sufferable, than
to right themselves by abolishing the forms to which they
are accustomed. but when a long train of abuses &
usurpations,· begun at a distinguished period, & pursuing
invariably the same object, evinces a design to ~~subject~~
reduce them to arbitrary power, it is their right, it is their
duty, to throw off such government & to provide new
guards for their future security. such has been the
patient sufferance of these colonies; & such is now the
necessity which constrains them to expunge their former
systems of government. the history of his present majesty
is a history of unremitting injuries and usurpations,
among which no one fact stands single or solitary to contradict the uniform tenor of the rest, all of which have
in direct object the establishment of an absolute tyranny
over these states. to prove this, let facts be submitted
to a candid world, for the truth of which we pledge a
faith yet unsullied[2] by falsehood.

he has refused his assent to laws the most wholesome and
necessary for the public good:

[1] Adams' copy reads "or transient."
[2] Adams' copy reads "as yet unsullied."

he has forbidden his governors to pass laws of immediate [1]
& pressing importance, unless suspended in their
operation till his assent should be obtained; and when
so suspended, he has neglected utterly to attend to
them.

he has refused to pass other laws for the accomodation
of large districts of people unless those people would
relinquish the right of representation_{in the legislature}, a right inestimable to them & formidable to tyrants only:

he has dissolved Representative houses repeatedly &
continually, for opposing with manly firmness his
invasions on the rights of the people:

~~he has dissolved,~~ he has refused for a long space of time
to cause others to be elected, whereby the legislative
powers, incapable of annihilation, have returned to the
people at large for their exercise, the state remaining
in the meantime exposed to all the dangers of invasion
from without, & convulsions within:

he has endeavored to prevent the population of these
states; for that purpose obstructing the laws for
naturalization of foreigners; refusing to pass others
to encourage their migrations hither; & raising the

[1] Adams' copy reads "an immediate."

conditions of new appropriations of lands:

he has suffered the administration of justice totally to
cease in some of these colonies, refusing his assent to
laws for establishing judiciary powers:

he has made our judges dependent on his will alone, for
the tenure of their offices, and amount of their salaries:

he has erected a multitude of new offices by a self-assumed
power, & sent hither swarms of officers to harrass our
people & eat out their substance:

he has kept among us in times of peace standing armies
& ships of war:

he has affected to render the military, independent of
& superior to the civil power:

he has combined with others to subject us to a jurisdiction
foreign to our constitutions[1] and unacknoleged by our
laws; giving his assent to their pretended acts of
legislation, for quartering large bodies of armed troops
among us;

    for protecting them by a mock-trial from punishment
    for any murders which they should commit on the in-
    habitants of these states;

    for cutting off our trade with all parts of the world;

[1] Adams' copy reads "constitution."

for imposing taxes on us without our consent;

for depriving us of the benefits of trial by jury;

for transporting us beyond seas to be tried for pretended offenses;

for taking away our charters, & altering fundamentally the forms of our governments;

for suspending our own legislatures & declaring themselves invested with power to legislate for us in all cases whatsoever:

he has abdicated government here, withdrawing his governors, & declaring us out of his allegiance & protection:

he has plundered our seas, ravaged our coasts, burnt our towns & destroyed the lives of our people:

he is at this time transporting large armies of foreign mercenaries to compleat the works of death, desolation & tyranny, already begun with circumstances of cruelty & perfidy unworthy the head of a civilized nation:

he has endeavored to bring on the inhabitants of our frontiers the merciless Indian savages, whose known rule of warfare is an undistinguished destruction of all ages, sexes, & conditions of existence:

he has incited treasonable insurrections of our fellow

citizens, with the allurements[1] of forfeiture & confiscation of our property:

he has waged cruel war against human nature itself,
violating it's most sacred rights[2] of life & liberty in
the persons of a distant people who never offended
him, captivating & carrying them into slavery in another
hemisphere, or to incur miserable death in their transportation thither. this piratical warfare, the opprobrium of *infidel* powers, is the warfare of the *Christian*
king of Great Britain. [determined to keep open a
market where MEN should be bought & sold,] he
has prostituted his negative for suppressing every
legislative attempt to prohibit or to restrain this
determining to keep open a market where MEN should be bought & sold:
execrable commerce ∧[3]: and that this assemblage of
horrors might want no fact of distinguished die, he is
now exciting those very people to rise in arms among us,
and to purchase that liberty of which *he* has deprived
them, by murdering the people upon whom *he* also obtruded them: thus paying off former crimes committed against the *liberties* of one people, with crimes which
he urges them to commit against the *lives* of another.

[1] Adams' copy reads "allurement."
[2] Adams' copy reads "right."
[3] Adams' copy reads "an execrable."

in every stage of these oppressions we have petitioned for redress in the most humble terms; our repeated petitions have been answered by repeated injury.[1] a prince whose character is thus marked by every act which may define a tyrant, is unfit to be the ruler of a people who mean to be free. future ages will scarce believe that the hardiness of one man, adventured within the short compass of twelve years only, on so many acts of tyranny without a mask, over a people fostered & fixed in principles [2] of liberty.

Nor have we been wanting in attentions to our British brethren. we have warned them from time to time of attempts by their legislature to extend a jurisdiction over these our states. we have reminded them of the circumstances of our emigration & settlement here, no one of which could warrant so strange a pretension: that these were effected at the expence of our own blood &

---

[1] The Rough Draft reads "injuries." But it is clear that the original form was "injury." The "y" has been erased and "ies" written in. All of the official texts read "injury," and all of Jefferson's own copies of the Declaration read "injury" except the one which he copied into his "Notes." It seems that Jefferson must have made this change after the Declaration was adopted, since it is unlikely that it would have been rejected by Congress if it had been in the report of the Committee of Five.

[2] Adams' copy reads "the principles."

treasure, unassisted by the wealth or the strength of Great Britain: that in constituting indeed our several forms of government, we had adopted one common king, thereby laying a foundation for perpetual league & amity with them: but that submission to their parliament was no part of our constitution, nor ever in idea, if history may be credited: and we appealed to their native justice & magnanimity, as well as to the ties of our common kindred to disavow these usurpations which were likely to interrupt our correspondence & connection. they too have been deaf to the voice of justice & of consanguinity, & when occasions have been given them, by the regular course of their laws, of removing from their councils the disturbers of our harmony, they have by their free election re-established them in power. at this very time too they are permitting their chief magistrate to send over not only soldiers of our common blood, but Scotch & foreign mercenaries to invade & deluge us in blood. these facts have given the last stab to agonizing affection, and manly spirit bids us to renounce forever these unfeeling brethren. we must endeavor to forget our former love for them, and to hold them as we hold the rest of mankind, enemies in war, in peace friends. we might have been a free & a great people together; but a communication of grandeur & of freedom it seems is below their dignity. be it so, since they will have it: the road to ~~glory &~~ happiness [& to glory] is open to us too; we will climb it ~~in a separately state,~~ [apart from them,] and acquiesce in the necessity which [de] pronounces our ~~everlasting Adieu!~~ eternal separation!

We therefore the representatives of the United States of America in General Congress assembled do, in the name & by authority[1] of the good people of these states, reject and renounce all allegiance & subjection to the kings of Great Britain & all others who may hereafter claim by, through, or under them; we utterly dissolve and break off all political connection which may have heretofore subsisted between us & the people or parliament of Great Britain; and finally we do assert and declare these colonies to be free and independent states, and that as free & independent states they shall hereafter have [full] power to levy war, conclude peace, contract alliances, establish commerce, & to do all other acts and things which independent states may of

[1] Adams' copy reads "the authority."

right do. And for the support of this declaration we mutually pledge to each other our lives, our fortunes, & our sacred honour.

Such, substantially, must have been the form of the Rough Draft when Jefferson first submitted it to Franklin. Between that day, whenever it was, and the 28 of June when the report of the Committee of Five was presented to Congress (it will presently appear how the report of the Committee can be approximately reconstructed), a total of twenty-six alterations were made in the Rough Draft. Twenty-three of these were changes in phraseology — two in Adams' hand, five in Franklin's, and sixteen apparently in Jefferson's. Besides these verbal changes, three entirely new paragraphs were added. If this be true, what are we to make of Jefferson's account of the matter in his letter to Madison? In this letter, quoted above, Jefferson says that having prepared the Draft he submitted it to "Dr. Franklin and Mr. Adams requesting their corrections; . . . their alterations were *two or three only, and merely verbal. I then wrote a fair copy, reported it to the committee, and from them, unaltered to the Congress.*" Jefferson here asserts that no changes were made in the Committee, and he implies that none except those in the handwriting of Franklin and Adams were made before the 'fair copy' was presented to the Committee. Either in the assertion or in the implication Jefferson's statement must be inaccurate.

Jefferson was probably right in the assertion that no changes were made in the Committee. He tells us that he submitted the Draft to Franklin and Adams first because they were the men whose corrections he most wished to have the benefit of. Jefferson, Franklin, and Adams were themselves a majority of the Committee; and if the draft was satisfactory to them it is quite likely that it would pass the Committee without change. Besides, there is no evidence to contradict Jefferson's statement on this point. What I suppose then is that the twenty-six alterations were all made before the 'fair copy' (or the Rough Draft, if Jefferson was mistaken in thinking there was a 'fair copy') was submitted to the Committee, and that these changes were the result of at least two, perhaps more, consultations between Jefferson and Franklin, and between Jefferson and Adams. Jefferson must have submitted the Draft to both Franklin and Adams at least twice, because the copy which Adams took contains only two of the five corrections which Franklin wrote into the Draft, and only one of the two which Adams himself wrote in. It was after Adams made his copy that he wrote in the second of his own corrections, that Franklin wrote in three of his corrections, and that Jefferson wrote in the three new paragraphs and sixteen verbal changes. Now there is nothing to show whether the corrections in Jefferson's hand were made before or after the later corrections by Franklin and Adams. I think we may assume that Jefferson, having written in three new paragraphs and sixteen verbal changes, would scarcely venture to make a 'fair copy' for the Committee, or, if there was no fair copy, would he be likely to present the Rough Draft thus corrected to the Committee, without having first submitted the Draft thus amended to Franklin and Adams for their final approval. Is it not then likely that it was on the occasion of this final submission of the corrected Draft to Franklin and Adams that they wrote in the corrections which appear in their hands but are not in the copy which Adams made?

The order of events in correcting the Rough Draft cannot in most respects be known; but I should guess that it was somewhat as follows. Having prepared the Draft, in which were eight slight verbal corrections made in process of composition, Jefferson first submitted it to Franklin. Franklin then wrote in one, and probably two, of the five corrections that appear in

his hand. Where the Draft read, "and amount of their salaries," Franklin changed it to read,
"and the amount & payment of their salaries." A second correction by Franklin was probably made at this time also. Jefferson originally wrote "reduce them to arbitrary power." Franklin's correction reads "reduce them under absolute Despotism." But Adams' copy reads "reduce them under absolute power," which is neither the original nor the corrected reading, but a combination of both. Adams may of course have made a mistake in copying (he made a number of slight errors in copying); or it may be that at this time Franklin wrote in "under absolute" in place of "to arbitrary," and that not until later, after Adams made his copy, was "power" crossed out and "Despotism" written in. In the original manuscript, "Despotism" appears to have been written with a different pen, or with heavier ink, than "under Absolute," as if written at a different time. At all events, not more than two of Franklin's five corrections had been made when Jefferson submitted the Draft to Adams. Adams then wrote in one of his two corrections: where Jefferson had written "for a long space of time," Adams added "after such dissolutions." Having made this correction, Adams made his copy

of the Draft as it then read, and, we may suppose, returned the Draft to Jefferson.

After receiving the Draft from Adams, Jefferson wrote in, at least the greater part of the
sixteen verbal changes, and three new paragraphs. The verbal changes he probably made
on his own initiative; they were mere improve-
ments in phraseology, such as would be likely
to occur to him upon rereading. He may like-
wise have added the three new paragraphs on
his own initiative; but I think it extremely
likely that Adams suggested the addition of the
paragraph about calling legislative bodies at
places remote from their public records. This
had actually occurred in Massachusetts, and
who more likely than Adams to remember it,
or to wish to have it included in the list of
grievances? This at least we know, that Jefferson wrote out on a slip of paper the following
paragraph:

he has called together legislative bodies at places unusual,

uncomfortable, & distant from the depository of their

public records, for the sole purpose of fatiguing them into

compliance with his measures.

The slip was then pasted at one end to the Rough
Draft at the place where occurs the paragraph
beginning, "he has dissolved Representative

houses repeatedly and continually."[1]   The two other paragraphs which Jefferson added after Adams returned the Draft are the one beginning, "for abolishing the free system of English laws,"[2] and the one beginning, "he has constrained others taken captives on the high seas."[3]

In whatever order these changes were made, and whether after only one or after several

---

[1] In the course of time a part of this slip was torn out and lost; but the rest of it, which is in two parts, was pasted down throughout, over, and largely concealing, the paragraph which reads: "he has dissolved Representative houses repeatedly & continually, for opposing with manly firmness his invasions on the rights of the people:" Of this paragraph, therefore, only a few words can now be seen on the Rough Draft; and of the paragraph written on the slip, only about two thirds can be seen. At this point the Rough Draft now reads as follows:

he has called together legislative bodies at places unusual, unco   t from
                                                                                                        lly] for opposing
the depository of their public records for the sole purpose of fatigui   nce
                                                                                             eople:
with his measures.

The word "continually," of which only the letters "lly" can now be seen, has the bracket because it was omitted by Congress, and Jefferson bracketed on the Rough Draft those parts omitted by Congress.

[2] This paragraph is written in at the bottom of page 2 of the Rough Draft; there was margin enough there to insert it by writing a very small hand and crowding the lines.

[3] This paragraph is written in on page 3 of the Rough Draft, between the paragraph beginning, "he has incited treasonable insurrections," and the paragraph beginning, "he has waged cruel war." Jefferson was able to crowd the new paragraph in because he left a pretty wide space between the lines when he wrote the Rough Draft; but the new paragraph had to be written so close and small that, even apart from the fact that this paragraph does not appear in Adams's copy, we should know it to be a later insertion.

conferences with Franklin or Adams, it may I think be assumed that Jefferson would submit the Rough Draft, after these changes were incorporated, to Franklin and Adams for their final approval before presenting the 'fair copy' (or the Rough Draft, if it was the Rough Draft) to the Committee. Now it may well have been at the time of this last inspection, after all other changes had been made, that Adams wrote in the second, and Franklin the last three of the corrections that appear in their handwriting. If this was in fact the order of events, it is not difficult to understand that Jefferson should have recalled the affair as he related it to Madison in 1823: "their alterations were two or three only, and merely verbal. I then wrote a fair copy, reported it to the Committee, & from them, unaltered to the Congress."

So far we have assumed that the three new paragraphs and the sixteen verbal changes in Jefferson's hand were written into the Rough Draft before it was submitted to the Committee of Five. But how do we know this, since Jefferson's 'fair copy' has not been preserved? How do we know these changes were not made by Congress? Fortunately, it is possible to reconstruct the report of the Committee of Five substantially as it must have read. We have a copy of the Declaration which Jefferson

made and sent to Richard H. Lee on the 8
of July, 1776, and which, in a letter to Lee
of that date, he says is the Declaration "as
originally framed."[1]   This copy, now possessed
by the American Philosophical Society, and
printed in facsimile in the *Proceedings* of the
society,[2] is quite obviously not the Declaration
'as originally framed' — that is, as Jefferson
framed it before submitting it to Franklin
and Adams for the first time — because it
differs strikingly from the copy which Adams
made.   It was probably made from the Rough
Draft at about the time that the Committee
of Five submitted its report to Congress; and
if that report was made, as Jefferson says, in
the form of a 'fair copy,' it is safe to assume
that it was intended to be a duplicate of the
fair copy.[3]   What Jefferson meant by the
phrase "as originally framed" was "as originally
reported."   This is confirmed by the fact that
Jefferson described another copy of the Declaration, and practically identical with the Lee
copy, by saying that it is the Declaration "as
originally reported."   This latter copy is the
one which he wrote into his "Notes," later

[1] *Writings of Thomas Jefferson* (Ford ed.), II, 59.
[2] *Proceedings of the American Philosophical Society*, XXXVII,
103–106.
[3] Hazelton, *op. cit.*, 306, 344.

printed as part of his *Autobiography.*[1]   Finally,
during the debates in Congress or afterward, Jefferson indicated on the Rough Draft the changes
made by Congress by bracketing the parts
omitted.   Thus the Lee copy, the copy in Jefferson's "Notes," and the Rough Draft exclusive
of the corrections made in connection with the
bracketed parts, furnish us with three texts
which were intended to conform to the report
of the Committee of Five.   The most reliable
of these texts is probably the Lee copy.   The
text given below is made by reproducing the
Rough Draft exclusive of all corrections that
do not appear in the Lee copy;   that is, it is
the Rough Draft as it must have read when
Jefferson made the Lee copy, assuming that he
made the Lee copy from the Rough Draft,
and made no errors in copying.   If Jefferson
made a 'fair copy' for the Committee, he may
of course have made the Lee copy from that
fair copy instead of from the Rough Draft.
In either case it can hardly be supposed that
he made any changes deliberately;   and if he
made any errors (he apparently made at least
one),[2] they were probably slight.   The corrections printed in roman are those which, being
incorporated in Adams' copy, I have assumed

[1] *Ibid.,* 171. *Writings of Thomas Jefferson* (Ford ed.), I, 29.
[2] See Page 170, Note 1.

were made by Jefferson in the process of composition before he first submitted the Draft to Franklin. All other corrections and additions are printed in italics. Where the reading of the Lee copy differs from that of the copy in the "Notes," excepting differences in punctuation and capitalization, I have noted the difference in footnotes.

THE ROUGH DRAFT

as it probably read when Jefferson

made the 'fair copy' which was pre-

sented to Congress as the report of

the Committee of Five.

A DECLARATION BY THE REPRESENTATIVES OF THE

UNITED STATES OF AMERICA, IN GENERAL

CONGRESS ASSEMBLED.

When in the course of human events it becomes neces-
sary for a ^one^ people to ^dissolve the political bands which have con-^ ~~advance from that subordination in~~
nected them with another, and to
~~which they have hitherto remained, & to~~ assume among
the powers of the earth the ^*separate and equal*^ ~~equal & independent~~ station

to which the laws of nature & of nature's god entitle them,

a decent respect to the opinions of mankind requires that

they should declare the causes which impel them to ^*the sep-*^ ~~the~~
aration
~~change.~~

We hold these truths to be ^self-evident; ~~sacred & undeniable;~~ that
all men are created equal ~~& independent;~~ that ~~from that~~ ^they are endowed by their
~~creator with equal rights, some of which are~~ ^rights; that
~~equal creation they derive in rights~~ inherent & inalienable ^
among ~~which~~ ^these ~~are the preservation of~~ life, ~~&~~ liberty, &
the pursuit of happiness; that to secure these ^rights ~~ends,~~
governments are instituted among men, deriving their
just powers from the consent of the governed; that
whenever any form of government ~~shall~~ becomes destructive of these ends, it is the right of the people to
alter or to abolish it, & to institute new government,
laying it's foundation on such principles & organizing
it's powers in such form, as to them shall seem most likely
to effect their safety & happiness. prudence indeed will
dictate that governments long established should not be
changed for light & transient causes: and accordingly all
experience hath shewn that mankind are more disposed to ·
suffer while evils are sufferable, than to right themselves
by abolishing the forms to which they are accustomed.
but when a long train of abuses & usurpations, begun
at a distinguished period, & pursuing invariably the
same object, evinces a design to ~~subject~~ reduce them
* *under absolute Despotism*
^~~to arbitrary power,~~ it is their right, it is their duty, to

* Dr. Franklin's handwriting

throw off such government & to provide new guards
for their future security. such has been the patient
sufferance of these colonies; & such is now the necessity
which constrains them to expunge their former systems
of government. the history of ~~his~~ present ~~majesty~~ is a

the . *king of Great Britain*

history of unremitting injuries and usurpations, among
which ~~no one fact stands single or solitary~~ to contradict

appears no solitary fact

the uniform tenor of the rest, ~~all of which~~ have in

but all

direct object the establishment of an absolute tyranny
over these states. to prove this, let facts be submitted
to a candid world, for the truth of which we pledge
a faith yet unsullied by falsehood.

he has refused his assent to laws the most wholesome and
necessary for the public good:

he has forbidden his governors to pass laws of immediate
& pressing importance, unless suspended in their operation till his assent should be obtained; and when so
suspended, he has neglected utterly[1] to attend to them.

he has refused to pass other laws for the accomodation

* Mr. Adams' handwriting

[1] The Rough Draft reads, "he has neglected ~~utterly.~~" The copy

utterly

in the "Notes" reads "utterly neglected." My belief is that this was
one of the corrections made by Congress which Jefferson neglected to
indicate as he commonly did such corrections, by bracketing the
omitted word.

of large districts of people unless those people would
relinquish the right of representation _{in the legislature}, a right inestimable to them & formidable to tyrants only:

he has called together legislative bodies at places unusual,
uncomfortable & distant from the depository of their
public records for the sole purpose of fatiguing them into
compliance with his measures:

he has dissolved, Representative houses repeatedly & continually, for opposing with manly firmness his invasions
on the rights of the people:

he has dissolved he has refused for a long space of time; *time after such dissolutions*
to cause others to be elected, whereby the legislative
powers, incapable of annihilation, have returned to the
people at large for their exercise, the state remaining in
the meantime exposed to all the dangers of invasion
from without, & convulsions within:

he has endeavored to prevent the population of these
states; for that purpose obstructing the laws for naturalization of foreigners; refusing to pass others to encourage their migrations hither; & raising the conditions
of new appropriations of lands:

he has suffered the administration of justice totally to

* Mr. Adams

cease in some of these ~~colonies~~, *states* refusing his assent to laws for establishing judiciary powers:

he has made our judges dependent on his will alone, for the tenure of their offices, and amount of their salaries:

he has erected a multitude of new offices by a self-assumed power, & sent hither swarms of officers to harrass our people & eat out their substance:

he has kept among us in times of peace standing armies & ships of war:

he has effected to render the military, independent of & superior to the civil power:

he has combined with others to subject us to a jurisdiction foreign to our constitutions and unacknoleged by our laws; giving his assent to their pretended ~~acts of~~ *acts of* legislation,

    for quartering large bodies of armed troops among us;

    for protecting them by a mock-trial from punishment for any murders they should commit on the inhabitants of these states;

† Dr. Franklin

for cutting off our trade with all parts of the world;

for imposing taxes on us without our consent;

for depriving us of the benefits of trial by jury;

for transporting us beyond seas to be tried for pretended offenses;

for abolishing the free system of English laws in a neighboring province, establishing therein an arbitrary government, and enlarging it's boundaries so as to render it at once an example & fit instrument for introducing the same absolute rule into these ~~colonies~~ states;

> valuable
> * abolishing our most ~~important~~ laws

for taking away our charters, ᴧ & altering fundamentally the forms of our governments;

for suspending our own legislatures & declaring themselves invested with power to legislate for us in all cases whatsoever:

he has abdicated government here, withdrawing his governors, & declaring us out of his allegiance & protection:

he has plundered our seas, ravaged our coasts, burnt our towns & destroyed the lives of our people:

he is at this time transporting large armies of foreign mercenaries to compleat the works of death, desolation & tyranny, already begun with circumstances of cruelty

* Dr. Franklin

& perfidy unworthy the head of a civilized nation:

he has endeavored to bring on the inhabitants of our frontiers the merciless Indian savages, whose known rule of warfare is an undistinguished destruction of all ages, sexes, & conditions of existence:

he has incited [1] treasonable insurrections of our fellow-citizens, with the allurements of forfeiture & confiscation of our property:

be has constrained others [2] *taken captives* ~~falling into his hands,~~ *on the high seas to bear arms against their country* ~~& to destroy & be destroyed by the brethren whom they love,~~ *to become the executioners of their friends & brethren, or to fall themselves by their hands.*

he has waged cruel war against human nature itself, violating it's most sacred rights of life & liberty in the persons of a distant people who never offended him, captivating & carrying them into slavery in another

---

[1] The copy in the "Notes" reads "excited."

[2] The copy in the "Notes" reads "our fellow citizens" in place of "others." This is the reading of the text as adopted by Congress; but as the change does not appear on the Rough Draft, I have assumed that this was a change made by Congress. The paragraph is written in the Rough Draft as here shown, following the paragraph beginning, "he has incited." Congress changed the order, placing the paragraph beginning "he has constrained" immediately following the one beginning "he is at this time transporting." The copy in the "Notes" follows the order adopted by Congress.

hemisphere, or to incur miserable death in their transportation thither. this piratical warfare, the opprobrium of *infidel* powers, is the warfare of the *Christian* king of Great Britain. *determined to keep open a market where MEN should be bought & sold*, he has prostituted his negative for suppressing every legislative attempt to prohibit or to restrain this execrable ~~determining to keep open a market where MEN should be bought & sold~~ commerce ∧ and that this assemblage of horrors might want no fact of distinguished die, he is now exciting those very people to rise in arms among us, and to purchase that liberty of which *he* has deprived them, by murdering the people upon whom *he* also obtruded them; thus paying off former crimes committed against the *liberties* of one people, with crimes which he urges them to commit against the *lives* of another.

in every stage of these oppressions we have petitioned for redress in the most humble terms; our repeated petitions have been answered $_∧^{* only}$ by repeated injury.[1] a prince whose character is thus marked by every act which may define a tyrant, is unfit to be the ruler of a people who mean to be free. future ages will scarce believe that the hardiness

* Dr. Franklin
[1] The Rough Draft reads "injuries." See above, p. 148, note 1.

of one man, adventured within the short compass of
build
~~to lay~~ *a foundation*[1] *so broad & undisguised for tyranny*
twelve years only, ⌃~~on so many acts of tyranny without~~
~~a mask,~~ over a people fostered & fixed in principles of
~~liberty.~~ *freedom.*

Nor have we been wanting in attentions to our British
brethren. we have warned them from time to time of
attempts by their legislature to extend a jurisdiction over
these our states. we have reminded them of the circumstances of our emigration & settlement here, no one
of which could warrant so strange a pretension: that
these were effected at the expence of our own blood &
treasure, unassisted by the wealth or the strength of
Great Britain: that in constituting indeed our several
forms of government, we had adopted one common king,
thereby laying a foundation for perpetual league & amity
with them: but that submission to their parliament was
no part of our constitution, nor ever in idea if history may
be credited: and we appealed to their native justice &
magnanimity as well as to the ties of our common kindred
to disavow these usurpations which were likely to interrupt
connection &
our ⌃correspondence ~~& connection.~~ they too have been

---

[1] The copy in the "Notes" reads "to lay a foundation."

deaf to the voice of justice & of consanguinity, & when occasions have been given them, by the regular course of their laws, of removing from their councils the disturbers of our harmony, they have by their free election re-established them in power. at this very time too they are permitting their chief magistrate to send over not only soldiers of our common blood, but Scotch & foreign mercenaries to invade & ~~deluge us in blood.~~ *destroy us* these facts have given the last stab to agonizing affection, and manly spirit bids us to renounce forever these unfeeling brethren. we must endeavor to forget our former love for them, and to hold them as we hold the rest of mankind, enemies in war, in peace friends. we might have been a free & a great people together; but a communication of grandeur & of freedom it seems is below their dignity. be it so, since they will have it: the road to ~~glory &~~ happiness *& to glory* is open to us too; we will climb it ~~in a separately state,~~[1] *apart from them*

---

* Dr. Franklin

[1] The Rough Draft reads,
   "we will ~~climb~~ it ~~in a separately state.~~" ~~must~~ tread apart from them

The text as adopted by Congress reads "we will climb it apart from them." The copy in the "Notes" is the only one which gives the reading "we will tread it apart from them." If the change from "climb" to "tread" was made before the Committee of Five submitted its and acquiesce in the necessity which ~~pronounces~~ ^{de} our ~~everlasting adieu!~~ eternal separation!

We therefore the representatives of the United States of America in General Congress assembled do, in the name & by authority of the good people of these states, reject and renounce all allegiance & subjection to the kings of Great Britain & all others who may hereafter claim by, through, or under them; we utterly dissolve ~~& break off~~ all political connection which may ~~have~~ *have* heretofore ^ subsisted between us & the people or parliament of Great Britain; and finally we do assert and declare[1] these colonies to be free and independent states, and that as free & independent states they ~~shall hereafter~~ *full* have ^

report, we must suppose that Jefferson made an error in the Lee copy and that Congress changed the "tread" back to "climb." This seems improbable. See below, pp. 199–201.

[1] Here I have followed the Rough Draft instead of the Lee copy. The Lee copy reads, "parliament or people . . . we do assert these colonies." There is no indication on the Rough Draft that 'people or parliament' was at any time changed to 'parliament or people,' nor is there any indication that 'and declare' was at any time omitted. Furthermore, the text adopted by Congress reads "publish and declare," which seems to indicate that the words 'and declare' were in the report of the Committee of Five. I assume therefore that the different reading of the Lee copy is the result of an error in copying. The copy which Jefferson incorporated in his "Notes" follows the reading of the Rough Draft; on the other hand, two other copies made by Jefferson, probably at the same time he made the Lee copy, follow the reading of the Lee copy. Cf. Hazelton, *op. cit.*, 177, 340.

power to levy war, conclude peace, contract alliances, establish commerce, & to do all other acts and things which independent states may of right do. And for the support of this declaration we mutually pledge to each other our lives, our fortunes, & our sacred honour.

The report of the Committee of Five, presented to Congress on June 28, was taken up four days later, debated on three successive days, and finally adopted with a number of amendments on the 4 of July. Since Congress sat, for these debates, in committee of the whole, the Journals give no account of either the debates or the amendments. Jefferson recorded, in his " Notes " taken at the time, a few details. In the " Notes " he says:

The pusillanimous idea that we had friends in England worth keeping terms with, still haunted the minds of many. For this reason those passages which conveyed censures on the people of England were struck out, lest they should give them offense. The clause too, reprobating the enslaving the inhabitants of Africa, was struck out in complaisance to South Carolina and Georgia, who had never attempted to restrain the importation of slaves, and who on the contrary still wished to continue it. Our Northern brethren also I believe felt a little tender under those censures; for tho' their people have very few slaves themselves yet they had been pretty considerable carriers of them to others.[1]

In a letter to Robert Walsh, December 4, 1818, Jefferson wrote as follows:

The words 'Scotch and other foreign auxillaries' excited the ire of a gentleman or two of that country. [Severe strictures on the British king, in negativing our repeated repeals of the law which permitted the importation of slaves, were disapproved by some Southern gentlemen, whose reflections were not yet matured to the full abhorrence of that traffic. Although the offensive expressions were immediately yielded, these gentlemen continued their depredations on other parts of the instrument.[2]

The Journal of Congress gives only the form of the Declaration as finally adopted. In what is called the 'rough Journal' the entry for July 4 is as follows:

Mr. Harrison reported that the Committee of the Whole Congress have agreed to a Declaration which he delivered in. The Declaration being read was agreed to as follows.[3]

---

[1] *Writings of Thomas Jefferson* (Ford ed.), I, 28.
[2] *Ibid.*, X, 119–120, note.
[3] Hazelton, *op. cit.*, 170, 306.

What follows in the 'rough Journal' is a printed copy of the Declaration — a copy printed by Dunlap by order of Congress and under the supervision of the Committee of Five. In what is known as the 'corrected Journal' the Declaration is written in.[1] The copy in the corrected Journal should, one would suppose, be the more authoritative text. Such seems, however, not to be the case. Apart from differences in punctuation and capitalization, in which the corrected Journal follows more closely the practice of Jefferson, the only differences in the two texts are the following: where the rough Journal reads, "for quartering large bodies of armed troops among us," the corrected Journal reads, "for quartering large bodies of troops among us"; and where the rough Journal reads, "they too have been deaf to the voice of justice and of consanguinity," the corrected Journal reads, "they too have been deaf to the voice of justice & consanguinity." The reading of the rough Journal in these two cases is the same as that of every other text we have, including the engrossed parchment copy. It seems clear, therefore, that these changes in the corrected Journal were not 'corrections' but simply inadvertent omissions. The copy in the rough Journal should thus be taken as the most au-

[1] *Ibid.*

thoritative text. If then, as I have assumed, the copy which Jefferson sent to Richard H. Lee is the nearest we can come to the 'fair copy' which was the report of the Committee of Five, a comparison of the Lee copy with the copy in the rough Journal will give us the changes made by Congress as accurately as it is possible to determine them. The text given below is the Lee copy, except for one reading in the last paragraph where Jefferson probably made an error in copying, with the parts omitted by Congress crossed out and the parts added interlined in italics.

THE DECLARATION OF INDEPENDENCE

(as it reads in the Lee copy, which is probably the same as the report of the Committee of Five, with parts omitted by Congress crossed out and the parts added interlined in italics.)

A DECLARATION BY THE REPRESENTATIVES OF THE UNITED STATES OF AMERICA IN GENERAL CONGRESS ASSEMBLED.

When in the course of human events it becomes necessary for one people to dissolve the political bands which have connected them with another, and to assume among

the powers of the earth the separate and equal station
to which the laws of nature and of nature's god entitle
them, a decent respect to the opinions of mankind requires that they should declare the causes which impel
them to the separation.

We hold these truths to be self-evident; that all men
are created equal; that they are endowed by their
Creator with ~~inherent and~~ ^{certain un}~~in~~alienable[1] rights; that,
among these are life, liberty, and the pursuit of happiness;
that to secure these rights, governments are instituted
among men, deriving their just powers from the consent
of the governed; that whenever any form of government
becomes destructive of these ends, it is the right of the
people to alter or to abolish it, and to institute new government, laying it's foundation on such principles, and organizing it's powers in such form as to them shall seem most
likely to effect their safety and happiness.   prudence

---

[1] The Rough Draft reads "[inherent &] ^{certain} inalienable." There is
no indication that Congress changed "inalienable" to "unalienable";
but the latter form appears in the text in the rough Journal, in the
corrected Journal, and in the parchment copy. John Adams, in making
his copy of the Rough Draft, wrote "unalienable." See above, p. 142,
note 2. Adams was one of the committee which supervised the printing
of the text adopted by Congress, and it may have been at his suggestion
that the change was made in printing. "Unalienable" may have been
the more customary form in the eighteenth century.

indeed will dictate that governments long established should not be changed for light & transient causes. and accordingly all experience hath shewn that mankind are more disposed to suffer, while evils are sufferable, than to right themselves by abolishing the forms to which they are accustomed. but when a long train of abuses and usurpations, ~~begun at a distinguished period &~~ pursuing invariably the same object, evinces a design to reduce them under absolute despotism, it is their right, it is their duty, to throw off such government, & to provide new guards for their future security. such has been the patient sufferance of these colonies, & such is now the necessity which constrains them to ~~expunge~~ _alter_ their former systems of government. the history of the present king of Great Britain is a history of ~~unremitting~~ _repeated_ injuries and usurpations, ~~among which appears no solitary fact to contradict the uniform tenor of the rest, but~~ all ~~have~~ _having_ in direct object the establishment of an absolute tyranny over these states. to prove this let facts be submitted to a candid world, ~~for the truth of which we pledge a faith yet unsullied by falsehood.~~

He has refused his assent to laws the most wholesome and
   necessary for the public good.

he has forbidden his governors to pass laws of immediate
& pressing importance, unless suspended in their operation till his assent should be obtained; and when so
suspended, he has ˄*utterly* neglected ~~utterly~~ to attend to them.

he has refused to pass other laws for the accomodation of
large districts of people, unless those people would
relinquish the right of representation in the legislature;
a right inestimable to them, & formidable to tyrants
only.

he has called together legislative bodies at places unusual,
uncomfortable, & distant from the depository of their
public records, for the sole purpose of fatiguing them
into compliance with his measures.

he has dissolved Representative houses repeatedly ~~& continually,~~ for opposing with manly firmness his invasions
on the rights of the people.

he has refused for a long time after such dissolutions to
cause others to be elected whereby the legislative
powers, incapable of annihilation, have returned to
the people at large for their exercise, the state remaining in the meantime exposed to all the dangers of invasion from without, & convulsions within.

he has endeavored to prevent the population of these

states; for that purpose obstructing the laws for naturalization of foreigners; refusing to pass others to
encourage their migrations hither; & raising the
conditions of new appropriations of lands.

he has ~~suffered~~ *obstructed* the administration of justice ~~totally to
cease in some of these states,~~ *by* refusing his assent to
laws for establishing judiciary powers.

he has made ~~our~~ judges dependent on his will alone, for
the tenure of their offices, and the amount & paiment
of their salaries.

he has erected a multitude of new offices ~~by a self assumed
power,~~ & sent hither swarms of officers to harrass our
people, and eat out their substance.

he has kept among us, in times of peace, standing armies
~~and ships of war,~~ without the consent of our legislatures.

he has affected to render the military independent of, &
superior to, the civil power.

he has combined with others to subject us to a jurisdiction
foreign to our ~~constitutions~~ and unacknoleged by
our laws; giving his assent to their acts of pretended
legislation for quartering large bodies of armed troops[1]
among us;

[1] The text in the corrected Journal reads "bodies of troops."

for protecting them by a mock-trial from punishment
for any murders which they should commit on the
inhabitants of these states;

for cutting off our trade with all parts of the world;

for imposing taxes on us without our consent;

for depriving us of the benefits of trial by jury; *in many cases*

for transporting us beyond seas to be tried for pretended offenses;

for abolishing the free system of English laws in a
neighboring province, establishing therein an arbitrary government, and enlarging it's boundaries so
as to render it at once an example & fit instrument
for introducing the same absolute rule into these
states;

for taking away our charters, abolishing our most
valuable laws, and altering fundamentally the forms
of our governments;

for suspending our own legislatures, & declaring themselves invested with power to legislate for us in all
cases whatsoever.

he has abdicated government here, ~~withdrawing his~~
~~governors,~~ & ^declaring us out of ~~his allegiance and~~
protection ^. *by* *and waging war against us*

he has plundered our seas, ravaged our coasts, burnt our towns, & destroyed the lives of our people.

he is at this time transporting large armies of foreign mercenaries, to compleat the works of death, desolation & tyranny, already begun with circumstances of cruelty & perfidy *scarcely paralleled in the most barbarous ages and totally* unworthy the head of a civilized nation.

he has *excited domestic insurrection amongst us and has* endeavored to bring on the inhabitants of our frontiers the merciless Indian savages, whose known rule of warfare is an undistinguished destruction of all ages, sexes, & conditions ~~of existence.~~

~~he has incited treasonable insurrections of our fellow citizens, with the allurements of forfeiture & confiscation of property.~~

he has constrained *our fellow citizens* ~~others,~~ taken captives on the high seas to bear arms against their country, to become the executioners of their friends & brethren, or to fall themselves by their hands.

~~he has waged cruel war against human nature itself, violating it's most sacred rights of life & liberty in the persons of a distant people, who never offended him, captivating and carrying them into slavery in another hemisphere, or to incur miserable death in their trans-~~

~~portation thither.   this piratical warfare, the oppro-~~
~~brium of *infidel* powers, is the warfare of the *Christian*~~
~~king of Great Britain.   determined to keep open a~~
~~market where MEN should be bought & sold, he has~~
~~prostituted his negative for suppressing every legisla-~~
~~tive attempt to prohibit or to restrain this execrable~~
~~commerce: and that this assemblage of horrors might~~
~~want no fact of distinguished die, he is now exciting~~
~~those very people to rise in arms among us, and to~~
~~purchase that liberty of which *he* has deprived them;~~
~~by murdering the people upon whom *he* also obtruded~~
~~them: thus paying off former crimes committed~~
~~against the *liberties* of one people, with crimes~~
~~which he urges them to commit against the *lives* of~~
~~another.~~

In every stage of these oppressions, we have petitioned for
redress in the most humble terms; our repeated petitions
have been answered only by repeated injury.   a prince
whose character is thus marked by every act which may
define a tyrant, is unfit to be the ruler of a _^ people ~~who~~
free
~~mean to be free.   future ages will scarce believe that the~~
~~hardiness of one man adventured within the short compass~~
~~of twelve years only to build a foundation, so broad and~~

~~undisguised, for tyranny over a people fostered and fixed~~
~~in principles of freedom.~~

Nor have we been wanting in attentions to our British
brethren. we have warned them from time to time of
attempts by their legislature to extend ~~a~~ *an unwarrantable* jurisdiction
over ~~these our states.~~ *us.* we have reminded them of the
circumstances of our emigration and settlement here, ~~no~~
~~one of which could warrant so strange a pretension:~~
~~that these were effected at the expence of our own blood~~
~~and treasure, unassisted by the wealth or the strength~~
~~of Great Britain: that in constituting indeed our several~~
~~forms of government, we had adopted one common king,~~
~~thereby laying a foundation for perpetual league and amity~~
~~with them: but that submission to their parliament was~~
~~no part of our constitution, nor ever in idea, if history~~
~~may be credited: and~~ we *have* appealed to their native justice
& magnanimity, ~~as well as to~~ *and we have conjured them by* the tyes of our common
kindred, to disavow these usurpations, which ~~were likely~~
~~to~~ *would inevitably* interrupt our connection *s* & correspondence. they too
have been deaf to the voice of justice and of consan-
guinity[1]; ~~and when occasions have been given them,~~
~~by the regular course of their laws, of removing from their~~

---

[1] The text in the corrected Journal reads "and consanguinity."

~~councils the disturbers of our harmony, they have by~~

~~their free election re-established them in power. at this~~

~~very time too, they are permitting their chief magistrate~~

~~to send over not only soldiers of our common blood, but~~

~~Scotch and foreign mercenaries to invade and destroy~~

~~us. these facts have given the last stab to agonizing~~

~~affection; and manly spirit bids us to renounce forever~~

therefore
~~these unfeeling brethren.~~ we must ‸ endeavor to forget our

~~former love for them, and to hold them as we hold the~~

~~rest of mankind, enemies in war, in peace friends. we~~

~~might have been a free & a great people together; but~~

~~a communication of grandeur and of freedom, it seems, is~~

~~below their dignity. be it so, since they will have it.~~

~~the road to happiness and to glory is open to us too;~~

~~we will climb it apart from them, and~~ acquiesce in the

and hold them, as we hold the rest
necessity which denounces our ~~eternal~~ separation ‸ ‡

of mankind, enemies in war, in peace friends.
We therefore the Representatives of the United states

appealing to the supreme judge of the world for the rectitude of our intentions
of America in General Congress assembled, ‸ do, in the

colonies, solemnly
name & by authority of the good people of these ‸ ~~states,~~

publish and declare, that these united colonies are and of right ought
~~reject and renounce all allegiance and subjection to the~~

to be free and independent states; that they are absolved from all allegi-
~~kings of Great Britain, & all others who may hereafter~~

ance to the British Crown, and that
~~claim by, through, or under them;—we utterly dissolve~~

all political connection ~~which may heretofore have sub-~~
~~sisted~~ between ~~us~~ _{them} and the _{state} ~~people or parliament~~ of Great

Britain ; ~~and finally we do assert and declare¹ these~~
is & ought to be totally dissolved;

~~colonies to be free and independent states,~~ & that as

free & independent states, they have full power to levy

war, conclude peace, contract alliances, establish com-

merce, & to do all other acts and things which independent

states may of right do.　And for the support of this dec-
with a firm reliance on the protection of divine providence,

laration, we mutually pledge to each other our lives,

our fortunes, and our sacred honor.

Contrary to a tradition early established and
long held, the Declaration was not signed by
the members of Congress on July 4.　Neither
the rough nor the corrected Journal shows any
signatures, except that the printed copy in the
rough Journal closes with these words, of course
in print: "Signed by order and in behalf of
the Congress, John Hancock, President."　The
secret domestic Journal for July 19 contains
the following entry: "Resolved that the Declaration passed on the 4th be fairly engrossed."
And in the margin there is added: "Engrossed
on parchment with the title and stile of "The
Unanimous Declaration of the 13 United States

¹ The reading here is not precisely that of the Lee copy. See p. 170,
note 1.

of America," and that the same when engrossed be signed by every member of Congress." On August 2 occurs the following entry: "The Declaration of Independence being engrossed and compared at the table was signed by the members." Certain members, being absent on the 2 of August, signed the engrossed copy at a later date.[1] The engrossed parchment copy, carefully preserved at Washington, is identical in phraseology with the copy in the rough Journal.[2] The paragraphing, except in one instance, is indicated by dashes; the capitalization and punctuation, following neither previous copies, nor reason, nor the custom of any age known to man, is one of the irremediable evils of life to be accepted with becoming resignation. Two slight errors in engrossing have been corrected by interlineation.

THE DECLARATION OF INDEPENDENCE

(as it reads in the parchment copy.)

THE UNANIMOUS DECLARATION OF THE THIRTEEN UNITED STATES OF AMERICA.

When in the Course of human events, it becomes necessary for one people to dissolve the political bands,

[1] For a discussion of this question, see Hazelton, *op. cit.*, Ch. 9.
[2] *Ibid.*, 208, 306.

which have connected them with another, and to assume among the powers of the earth, the separate and equal station to which the Laws of Nature and of Nature's God entitle them, a decent respect to the opinions of mankind requires that they should declare the causes which impel them to the separation.⎦— We hold these truths to be self-evident, that all men are created equal, that they are endowed by their Creator with certain unalienable Rights, that among these are Life, Liberty and the pursuit of Happiness. — That to secure these rights, Governments are instituted among Men, deriving their just powers from the consent of the governed, — That whenever any Form of Government becomes destructive of these ends, it is the Right of the People to alter or to abolish it, and to institute new Government, laying its foundation on such principles and organizing its powers in such form, as to them shall seem most likely to effect their Safety and Happiness.⎦ Prudence, indeed, will dictate that Governments long established should not be changed for light and transient causes; and accordingly all experience hath shewn, that mankind are more disposed to suffer, while evils are sufferable, than to right themselves by abolishing the forms to which they are

accustomed. But when a long train of abuses and usurpations, pursuing invariably the same Object evinces a
design to reduce them under absolute Despotism, it is
their right, it is their duty, to throw off such Government,
and to provide new Guards for their future security. —
Such has been the patient sufferance of these Colonies;
and such is now the necessity which constrains them to
alter their former Systems of Government. The history
of the present King of Great Britain is a history of repeated injuries and usurpations, all having in direct
object the establishment of an absolute Tyranny over
these States. To prove this, let Facts be submitted to
a candid world. —He has refused his Assent to Laws,
the most wholesome and necessary for the public good. —
He has forbidden his Governors to pass Laws of immediate
and pressing importance, unless suspended in their operation till his Assent should be obtained; and when so suspended, he has utterly neglected to attend to them.—
He has refused to pass other Laws for the accommodation
of large districts of people, unless those people would
relinquish the right of Representation in the Legislature,
a right inestimable to them and formidable to tyrants
only. — He has called together legislative bodies at

places unusual, uncomfortable, and distant from the depository of their public Records, for the sole purpose of fatiguing them into compliance with his measures. — He has dissolved Representative Houses repeatedly, for opposing with manly firmness his invasions on the rights of the people. — He has refused for a long time, after such dissolutions, to cause others to be elected; whereby the Legislative powers, incapable of Annihilation, have returned to the People at large for their exercise; the State remaining in the meantime exposed to all the dangers of invasion from without, and convulsions within. — He has endeavoured to prevent the population of these States; for that purpose obstructing the Laws for Naturalization of Foreigners; refusing to pass others to encourage their migrations hither, and raising the conditions of new Appropriations of Lands. — He has obstructed the Administration of Justice, by refusing his Assent to Laws for establishing Judiciary powers. — He has made Judges dependent on his Will alone, for the tenure of their offices, and the amount and payment of their salaries. — He has erected a multitude of New Offices, and sent hither swarms of Officers to harrass our people, and eat out their substance. — He has kept among us, in times of peace, Standing Armies without the Consent of our legislatures. — He has affected to render the Military independent of and superior to the Civil power. — He has combined with others to subject us to a jurisdiction foreign to our constitution, and unacknowledged by our laws; giving his Assent to their Acts of pretended Legislation. — For quartering large bodies of armed troops among us: — For protecting them, by a mock Trial, from punishment for any Murders which they should commit on the Inhabitants of these States: — For cutting off our Trade with all parts of the world: — For imposing Taxes on us without our Consent: — For depriving us in many cases, of the benefits of Trial by Jury: — For transporting us beyond Seas to be tried for pretended offenses: — For abolishing the free System of English Laws in a neighboring Province, establishing therein an Arbitrary government, and enlarging its Boundaries so as to render it at once an example and fit instrument for introducing the same absolute rule into these Colonies: — For taking away our Charters, abolishing our most valuable Laws, and altering fundamentally the Forms of our Governments: — For suspending our own Legislatures, and declaring themselves invested with power to legislate for us in all cases whatsoever. — He has abdicated Government here, by declaring us out of his Protection and waging War against us. — He has plundered our seas, ravaged our Coasts, burnt our towns, and destroyed the lives of our people. — He is at this time transporting large Armies of foreign Mercenaries to compleat the works of death, desolation and tyranny, already begun with circumstances of Cruelty & perfidy scarcely paralleled in the most barbarous ages, and totally unworthy the Head of a civilized nation. — He has constrained our fellow Citizens taken Captive on the high Seas to bear Arms against their Country, to become the executioners of their friends and Brethren, or to fall themselves by their Hands. — He has excited domestic insurrections amongst us, and has endeavoured to bring on the inhabitants of our frontiers, the merciless Indian Savages, whose known rule of warfare, is an undistinguished destruction of all ages, sexes and conditions. In every stage of these Oppressions We have Petitioned for Redress in the most humble terms: Our repeated Petitions have been answered ˄ᵒⁿˡʸ by repeated injury. A Prince whose character is thus marked by every act which may define a Tyrant, is unfit to be the ruler of a free people. Nor have We been wanting in attentions to our Brittish brethren. We have warned them from time to time of attempts by their legislature to extend an unwarrantable jurisdiction over us. We have reminded them of the circumstances of our emigration and settlement here. We have appealed to their native justice and magnanimity, and we have conjured them by the ties of our common kindred to disavow these usurpations, which would inevitably interrupt our connections and correspondence. They too have been deaf to the voice of justice and of consanguinity. We must, therefore, acquiesce in the necessity, which denounces our Separation, and hold them, as we hold the rest of mankind, Enemies in War, in Peace Friends. —

We, therefore, the Representatives of the united States of America, in General Congress, Assembled, appealing to the Supreme Judge of the world for the rectitude of our intentions do, in the Name, and by Authority of the good People of these Colonies, solemnly publish and declare, That these United Colonies are, and of Right ought to be Free and Independent States; that they are Absolved from all Allegiance to the British Crown, and that all political connection between them and the State of Great Britain, is and ought to be totally dissolved; and that as

Free and Independent States, they have full Power to levy War, conclude Peace, contract Alliances, establish Commerce, and to do all other Acts and Things which Independent States may of right do. — And for the support of this Declaration, with a firm reliance on the protection of divine Providence, we mutually pledge to each other our Lives, our Fortunes and our sacred Honor.

The signatures on the parchment copy, of which only a few are now legible, are given below.

John Hancock.	Fran? Lewis.
Samuel Chase.	Lewis Morris.
W? Paca.	Rich? Stockton.
Tho? Stone.	Jn° Witherspoon.
Charles Carroll of Carrollton.	Fra? Hopkinson.
George Wythe.	John Hart.
Richard Henry Lee.	Abra Clark.
Th Jefferson.	Josiah Bartlett.
Benj? Harrison.	W? Whipple.
Tho? Nelson jr.	Sam¹ Adams.
Francis Lightfoot Lee.	John Adams.
Carter Braxton.	Rob? Treat Paine.
Rob? Morris.	Elbridge Gerry.

Benjamin Rush.

Benjᵃ Franklin.

John Morton.

Geo Clymer.

Jaˢ Smith.

Geo. Taylor.

James Wilson.

Geo. Ross.

Caesar Rodney.

Geo Read.

Tho M: Kean.

Wᵐ Floyd.

Phil. Livingston.

Arthur Middleton.

Button Gwinnett.

Step Hopkins.

William Ellery.

Roger Sherman.

Samˡ Huntington.

Wᵐ Williams.

Oliver Wolcott.

Matthew Thornton.

Wᵐ Hooper.

Joseph Hewes.

John Penn.

Edward Rutledge.

Thoˢ Heyward Junʳ

Thomas Lynch Junʳ

Lyman Hall.

Geo Walton.

CHAPTER V

THE LITERARY QUALITIES OF THE DECLARATION

JEFFERSON was chosen to draft the Declaration because he was known to possess a "masterly pen." There were perhaps other reasons, but this was the chief one. When he came to Congress in 1775, "he brought with him," says John Adams, "a reputation for literature, science, and a happy talent for composition. Writings of his were handed about remarkable for the peculiar felicity of expression."[1] *Peculiar felicity of expression* — the very words which one would perhaps choose to sum up the distinguishing characteristics of Jefferson's style.

Like many men who write with felicity, Jefferson was no orator. He rarely, if ever, made a speech. "During the whole time I sat with him in Congress," John Adams says, "I never heard him utter three sentences together" — that is, on the floor of Congress; in committees and in conversation he was, on the contrary, "prompt, frank, explicit, and de-

[1] *Works of John Adams*, II, 514.

cisive."[1] It might seem that a man who can write effectively should be able to speak effectively. It sometimes happens. But one whose ear is sensitive to the subtler, elusive harmonies of expression, one who in imagination hears the pitch and cadence and rhythm of the thing he wishes to say before he says it, often makes a sad business of public speaking because, painfully aware of the imperfect felicity of what has been uttered, he forgets what he ought to say next. He instinctively wishes to cross out what he has just said, and say it over again in a different way — and this is what he often does, to the confusion of the audience. In writing he can cross out and rewrite at leisure, as often as he likes, until the sound and the sense are perfectly suited — until the thing *composes*. The reader sees only the finished draft.

Not that Jefferson wrote with difficulty, constructing his sentences with slow and painful effort. One who, as an incident to a busy public career, wrote so much and so well, must have written with ease and rapidity. But Jefferson, as the original drafts of his papers show, revised and corrected his writings with care, seeking, yet without wearing his soul threadbare in the search, for the better word, the happier phrase, the smoother transition. His style

[1] *Ibid.*, 511-514.

has not indeed the achieved perfection, the impeccable surface, of that of a master-craftsman like Flaubert, or Walter Pater; but neither has it the objectivity, the impersonal frigidity of writing that is perhaps too curiously and deliberately integrated, too consciously made. Having something to say, he says it, with as much art as may be, yet not solely for the art's sake, aiming rather at the ease, the simplicity, the genial urbanity of cultivated conversation. The grace and felicity of his style have a distinctly personal flavor, something Jeffersonian in the implication of the idea, or in the beat and measure of the words. Franklin had equal ease, simplicity, felicity; but no one who knows the writings of Franklin could attribute the Declaration to him. Jefferson communicated an undefinable yet distinctive quality to the Declaration which makes it his.

The Declaration is filled with these felicities of phrase which bear the stamp of Jefferson's mind and temperament: *a decent respect to the opinions of mankind; more disposed to suffer, while evils are sufferable, than to right themselves by abolishing the forms to which they are accustomed; for the sole purpose of fatiguing them into compliance with his measures; sent hither swarms of officers to harrass our people and eat out their substance; hold them as we hold the rest of man-*

kind, enemies in war, in peace friends. There are some sentences in the Declaration which are more than felicitous. The closing sentence, for example, is perfection itself. Congress amended the sentence by including the phrase, "with a firm reliance upon the protection of divine Providence." It may be that Providence always welcomes the responsibilities thrust upon it in times of war and revolution; but personally, I like the sentence better as Jefferson wrote it. "And for the support of this Declaration we mutually pledge to each other our lives, our fortunes, and our sacred honor." It is true (assuming that men value life more than property, which is doubtful) that the statement violates the rhetorical rule of climax; but it was a sure sense that made Jefferson place 'lives' first and 'fortunes' second. How much weaker if he had written "our fortunes, our lives, and our sacred honor"! Or suppose him to have used the word 'property' instead of 'fortunes!' Or suppose him to have omitted 'sacred!' Consider the effect of omitting any of the words, such as the last two 'ours' — "our lives, fortunes, and sacred honor." No, the sentence can hardly be improved.

There are probably more of these Jeffersonian felicities in the Declaration than in any other writing by him of equal length. Jefferson

realized that, if the colonies won their independence, this would prove to be a public document
of supreme importance; and the Rough Draft
(which may not be the first one) bears ample
evidence of his search for the right word, the
right phrasing.   In the opening sentence, not
at all bad as it originally stood, there are four
corrections.   The first part of the second paragraph seems to have given him much trouble.
The Rough Draft reads as follows:

> We hold these truths to be ~~sacred & undeniable;~~ ^{self-evident} that
> all men are created equal ~~& independent;~~ that ~~from~~ they are endowed by their
> ~~that equal creation they derive in rights~~ creator with ~~equal rights some of which are~~ inherent &
> inalienable among ~~which~~ are ~~the preservation of~~ life, rights; that these
> ~~&~~ liberty, & the pursuit of happiness.

When Jefferson submitted the draft to Adams
the only correction which he had made was to
write 'self-evident' in place of 'sacred & undeniable.'   It is interesting to guess why, on a
later reading, the other changes were made.   I
suspect that he erased '& independent' because,
having introduced 'self-evident,' he did not like
the sound of the two phrases both closing with
'dent.'   The phrase 'they are endowed by their
creator' is obviously much better than 'from
that equal creation': but this correction, as

he first wrote it, left an awkward wording: 'that they are endowed by their creator with equal rights some of which are inherent & inalienable among which are.' Too many 'which ares'; and besides, why suppose that some rights given by the creator were inherent and some not? Thus we get the form, which is so much stronger, as well as more agreeable to the ear: 'that they are endowed by their creator with inherent & inalienable rights.' Finally, why say 'the preservation of life'? If a man has a right to life, the right to preserve life is manifestly included.

Again, take the close of the last paragraph but one. The Rough Draft gives the following reading:

The road to ~~glory &~~ happiness^(& to glory)is open to us too; we will climb it^ ~~must~~ tread (apart from them) ~~in a separately state.~~

The phrase 'to happiness & to glory' is better than 'to glory & happiness.' Placing "glory" before "happiness" might imply that the first aim of the colonists was glory, and that their happiness would come as an incident to the achievement of glory. What needed to be expressed was the idea that the colonists were defending the natural right to happiness, and that the vindication of this inherent human right would confer glory upon them. Did Jefferson, in making the change, reason thus? Probably not. Upon reading it over he doubtless instinctively felt that by placing 'happiness' first and repeating the 'to' he would take the flatness out of a prosaic phrase. As for the latter part of the sentence, Jefferson evidently first wrote it: 'climb it in a separate state.' Not liking the word "state," he erased 'state' and 'in a' and added '-ly' to 'separate': so that it read: 'we will climb it separately.' But no, on second thought, that is not much better. 'Climb it apart from them' — that would do. So apparently it read when the Declaration was adopted, since 'climb' and not 'tread' is the reading of all but one of the copies, including the text finally adopted. It may be that Jefferson made the change during the debates in Congress, and then thought better of it, or neglected to get the change incorporated in the final text. There is another correction in the Rough Draft which does not appear in the final form of the Declaration. "Our repeated petitions have been answered only by repeated injury" — so the Declaration reads; but in the Rough Draft the 'injury' has been changed to 'injuries.' This is manifestly better; and as one can hardly suppose Congress would have preferred 'injury' to 'injuries,' it is probable that the change was made after the Declaration was adopted. Jefferson had something of the artist's love of perfection for its own sake, the writer's habit of correcting a manuscript even after it has been published.

Apart from the peculiar felicities of phrasing, what strikes one particularly in reading the Declaration as a whole is the absence of declamation. Everything considered, the Declaration is brief, free of verbiage, a model of clear, concise, and simple statement. In 1856 Rufus Choate referred to it as "that passionate and eloquent manifesto," made up of "glittering and sounding generalities of natural right."[1] Eloquent the Declaration frequently is, in virtue of a certain high seriousness with which Jefferson contrived to invest what was ostensibly a direct and simple statement of fact. Of all words in the language, 'passionate' is the one which is least applicable to Jefferson or to his writings. As to 'generalities,' the Declaration contains relatively few; and if those few are 'glittering and sounding' it is in their substance and not in their form that they are so. You may not believe

that all men are created equal; that they are endowed

by their creator with certain unalienable rights; that

[1] Letter to E. W. Farley, Aug. 9, 1856; Brown, S. G. *Life of Rufus Choate*, 324, 326.

among these are life, liberty, and the pursuit of happiness; that to secure these rights governments are instituted among men, deriving their just powers from the consent of the governed; that whenever any form of government becomes destructive of these ends, it is the right of the people to alter or to abolish it, and to institute new government, laying its foundations on such principles, and organizing its powers in such form, as to them shall seem most likely to effect their safety and happiness.

You may not believe this; but if you do believe it, as Jefferson and his contemporaries did, you would find it difficult to say it more concisely; in words more direct, simple, precise, and appropriate; with less of passionate declamation, of rhetorical magniloquence, or of verbal ornament. The second paragraph of the Declaration of Independence reminds one of Lincoln's Gettysburg Address in its unimpassioned simplicity of statement. It glitters as much, or as little, as that famous document.

Logical sequence and structural unity are not always essential to good writing; but the rambling and discursive method would scarcely be appropriate to a declaration of independence. Jefferson's declaration, read casually, seems not to possess a high degree of unity. Superficially considered, it might easily strike one as the result of an uneasy marriage of convenience between an abstract philosophy of government and certain concrete political grievances. But in truth the Declaration is built up around a single idea, and its various parts are admirably chosen and skilfully disposed for the production of a particular effect. The grievances against the king occupy so much space that one is apt to think of them as the main theme. Such is not the case. The primary purpose of the Declaration was to convince a candid world that the colonies had a moral and legal right to separate from Great Britain. This would be difficult to do, however many and serious their grievances might be, if the candid world was to suppose that the colonies were politically subordinate to the British government in the ordinary sense. It is difficult to justify rebellion against established political authority. Accordingly, the idea around which Jefferson built the Declaration was that the colonists were not rebels against established political authority, but a free people maintaining long established and imprescriptible rights against a usurping king. The effect which he wished to produce was to leave a candid world wondering why the colonies had so long submitted to the oppressions of this king.

The major premise from which this conclusion

is derived is that every 'people' has a natural right to make and unmake its own government; the minor premise is that the Americans are a 'people' in this sense. In establishing themselves in America, the people of the colonies exercised their natural rights to frame governments suited to their ideas and conditions; but at the same time they voluntarily retained a union with the people of Great Britain by professing allegiance to the same king. From this allegiance they might at any time have withdrawn; if they had not so withdrawn it was because of the advantages of being associated with the people of Great Britain; if they now proposed to withdraw, it was not because they now any less than formerly desired to maintain the ancient association, but because the king by repeated and deliberate actions had endeavored to usurp an absolute authority over them contrary to every natural right and to long established custom. The minor premise of the argument is easily overlooked because it is not explicitly stated in the Declaration — at least not in its final form. To have stated it explicitly would perhaps have been to bring into too glaring a light certain incongruities between the assumed premise and known historical facts. The rôle of the list of grievances against the king is to make the assumed premise emerge, of its own accord as it were, from a carefully formulated but apparently straightforward statement of concrete historical events. From the point of view of structural unity, the rôle which the list of grievances plays in the Declaration is a subordinate one; its part is to exhibit the historical circumstances under which the colonists, as a 'free people,' had thrust upon them the high obligation of defending the imprescriptible rights of all men.

Although occupying a subordinate place in the logical structure, the list of grievances is of the highest importance in respect to the total effect which the Declaration aims to produce. From this point of view, the form and substance of these paragraphs constitute not the least masterly part of the Declaration. It is true, books upon rhetoric warn the candidate for literary honors at all hazards to avoid monotony; he ought, they say, to seek a pleasing variety by alternating long and short sentences; and while they consider it correct to develop a single idea in each paragraph, they consider it inadvisable to make more than one paragraph out of a single sentence. These are no doubt good rules, for writing in general; but Jefferson violated them all, perhaps because he was writing something in particular. Of set purpose, throughout this part of the Declaration, he began each charge against the king with 'he has': 'he has refused his assent'; 'he has forbidden his governors'; 'he has refused to pass laws'; 'he has called together legislative bodies'; 'he has refused for a long time.' As if fearing that the reader might not after all notice this oft-repeated 'he has,' Jefferson made it still more conspicuous by beginning a new paragraph with each 'he has.' To perform thus is not to be 'literary' in a genteel sense; but for the particular purpose of drawing an indictment against the king it served very well indeed. Nothing could be more effective than these brief, crisp sentences, each one the bare affirmation of a malevolent act. Keep your mind on the king, Jefferson seems to say; he is the man: '*he has refused*'; '*he has forbidden*'; '*he has combined*'; '*he has incited*'; '*he has plundered*'; '*he has abdicated.*' I will say he has.

These hard, incisive sentences are all the more effective as an indictment of the king because of the sharp contrast between them and the paragraphs, immediately preceding and following, in which Jefferson touches upon the sad state of the colonists. In these paragraphs there is something in the carefully chosen words, something in the falling cadence of the sentences, that conveys a mournful, almost a funereal, sense of evils apprehended and long forefended but now unhappily realized. Consider the phrases which give tone and pitch to the first two paragraphs: 'when in the course of human events'; 'decent respect to the opinions of mankind'; 'all experience hath shewn'; 'suffer while evils are sufferable'; 'forms to which they are accustomed'; 'patient sufferance of these colonies'; 'no solitary fact to contradict the uniform tenor of the rest.' Such phrases skilfully disposed have this result, that the opening passages of the Declaration give one the sense of fateful things impending, of hopes defeated and injuries sustained with unavailing fortitude. The contrast in manner is accentuated by the fact that whereas the king is represented as exclusively aggressive, the colonists are represented as essentially submissive. In this drama the king alone acts — he conspires, incites, plunders; the colonists have the passive part, never lifting a hand to burn stamps or destroy tea; they suffer while evils are sufferable. It is a high literary merit of the Declaration that by subtle contrasts Jefferson contrives to conjure up for us a vision of the virtuous and long-suffering colonists standing like martyrs to receive on their defenseless heads the ceaseless blows of the tyrant's hand.

Like many men with a sense for style, Jefferson, although much given to polishing and correcting his own manuscripts, did not always welcome changes which others might make. Congress discussed his draft for three successive days. What uncomplimentary remarks the members may have made is not known; but it is known that in the end certain paragraphs were greatly changed and others omitted altogether. These 'depredations' — so he speaks of them — Jefferson did not enjoy: but we may easily console ourselves for his discomfiture since it moved the humane Franklin to tell him a story. Writing in 1818, Jefferson says:

I was sitting by Dr. Franklin, who perceived that I was not insensible to these mutilations. 'I have made it a rule,' said he, ' whenever in my power, to avoid becoming the draughtsman of papers to be reviewed by a public body. I took my lesson from an incident which I will relate to you. When I was a journeyman printer, one of my companions, an apprentice Hatter, having served out his time, was about to open shop for himself. His first concern was to have a handsome signboard, with a proper inscription. He composed it in these words: 'John Thompson, Hatter, makes and sells hats for ready money,' with a figure of a hat subjoined. But he thought he would submit it to his friends for their amendments. The first he shewed it to thought the word 'hatter' tautologous, because followed by the words 'makes hats' which shew he was a hatter. It was struck out. The next observed that the word 'makes' might as well be omitted, because his customers would not care who made the hats. If good and to their mind, they would buy, by whomsoever made. He struck it out. A third said he thought the words 'for ready money' were useless as it was not the custom of the place to sell on credit. Every one who purchased expected to pay. They were parted with, and the inscription now stood 'John Thompson sells hats.' '*Sells* hats' says his next friend? Why nobody will expect you to give them away. What then is the use of that word? It was stricken out, and 'hats' followed it, the rather, as there was one painted on the board. So his inscription was reduced ultimately to 'John Thompson' with the figure of a hat subjoined.'[1]

Jefferson's colleagues were not so ruthless as the friends of John Thompson; and on the whole it must be said that Congress left the Declaration better than it found it. The few verbal changes that were made improved the phraseology, I am inclined to think, in every case.

[1] *Writings of Thomas Jefferson* (Ford ed.), X, 120.

Where Jefferson wrote: "He has erected a multitude of new offices by a self-assumed power, and sent hither swarms of officers to harrass our people and eat out their substance," Congress cut out the phrase, "by a self-assumed power." Again, Jefferson's sentence, "He has abdicated government here, withdrawing his governors, and declaring us out of his allegiance and protection," Congress changed to read, "He has abdicated government here by declaring us out of his protection and waging war against us." Is not the phraseology of Congress, in both cases, more incisive, and does it not thus add something to that very effect which Jefferson himself wished to produce?

Aside from merely verbal changes, Congress rewrote the final paragraph, cut out the greater part of the paragraph next to the last, and omitted altogether the last of Jefferson's charges against the king. The final paragraph as it stands is certainly much stronger than in its original form. The Declaration was greatly strengthened by using, for the renunciation of allegiance, the very phraseology of the resolution of July 2, by which Congress had officially decreed that independence which it was the function of the Declaration to justify. It was no doubt for this reason mainly that Congress rewrote the paragraph; but the revision had in addition the merit of giving to the final paragraph, what such a paragraph especially needed, greater directness and assurance. In its final form, the Declaration closes with the air of accepting the issue with confident decision.

In cutting out the greater part of the next to the last paragraph, Congress omitted, among other things, the sentence in which Jefferson formulated, not directly indeed but by allusion, that theory of the constitutional relation of the colonies to Great Britain which is elsewhere taken for granted: "We have reminded them [our British brethren] . . . that in constituting indeed our several forms of government, we had adopted one common king; thereby laying a foundation for perpetual league and amity with them; but that submission to their parliament was no part of our constitution, nor ever in idea, if history may be credited." Perhaps the Declaration would have been strengthened by including an explicit formulation of this theory. But if the theory was to be expressly formulated at all, Jefferson was unfortunate both in the form and in the order of the statement. Unfortunate in the form, which is allusive, and in the last phrase ambiguous — "Nor ever in idea, if history may be credited." Unfortunate in the order, because, if the theory was to be expressly formulated at all, its formulation should manifestly have preceded the list of charges against the king. In general, this paragraph, as originally written, leaves one with the feeling that the author, not quite aware that he is done, is beginning over again. In the form adopted, it is an admirable brief prelude to the closing paragraph.

The last of Jefferson's charges against the king was what John Adams called the "vehement philippic against negro slavery."[1]

He has waged cruel war against human nature itself, violating its most sacred rights of life and liberty in the persons of a distant people who never offended him, captivating and carrying them into slavery in another hemisphere, or to incur miserable death in their transportation thither. This piratical warfare, the opprobrium of *infidel* powers, is the warfare of the *Christian* king of Great Britain. Determined to keep open a market where MEN should be bought and sold, he has prostituted his negative for suppressing every legislative attempt to prohibit or to restrain this execrable commerce; and that this assemblage of horrors might want no fact of distinguished die, he is now exciting these very people to rise in arms among us, and to purchase that liberty

[1] *Works of John Adams*, II, 514.

of which *he* deprived them, by murdering the people upon whom *he* also obtruded them; thus paying off former crimes committed against the *liberties* of one people, with crimes which he urges them to commit against the *lives* of another.

Congress omitted this passage altogether. I am glad it did. One does not expect a declaration of independence to represent historical events with the objectivity and exactitude of a scientific treatise; but here the discrepancy between the fact and the representation is too flagrant. Expecially, in view of the subsequent history of the slave trade, and of slavery itself, without which there would have been no slave trade, these charges against the king lose whatever plausibility, slight enough at best, they may have had at the time. But I have quoted this passage in full once more, not on account of its substance but on account of its form, which is interesting, and peculiarly significant in its bearing upon Jefferson's qualities and limitations as a writer. John Adams thought it one of the best parts of the Declaration. It is possible that Jefferson thought so too. He evidently gave much attention to the wording of it. But to me, even assuming the charges against the king to be true, it is the part of the

Declaration in which Jefferson conspicuously failed to achieve literary excellence.

The reason is, I think, that in this passage Jefferson attempted something which he was temperamentally unfitted to achieve. The passage was to have been the climax of the charges against the king; on its own showing of facts it imputes to him the most inhuman acts, the basest motives; its purpose, one supposes, is to stir the reader's emotions, to make him feel a righteous indignation at the king's acts, a profound contempt for the man and his motives. Well, the passage is clear, precise, carefully balanced. It employs the most tremendous words — "murder," "piratical warfare," "prostituted," "miserable death." But in spite of every effort, the passage somehow leaves us cold; it remains, like all of Jefferson's writing, calm and quiescent; it lacks warmth; it fails to lift us out of our equanimity. There is in it even (something rare indeed in Jefferson's writings) a sense of labored effort, of deliberate striving for an effect that does not come.

This curious effect, or lack of effect, is partly due to the fact that the king's base actions are presented to us in abstract terms. We are not permitted to see George III. George III does not repeal a statute of South Carolina in order that Sambo may be sold at the port of Charleston. No, the Christian king wages "cruel war against human nature," he prostitutes "his negative for the suppression of every legislative attempt to prohibit or to restrain this execrable commerce." We have never a glimpse of poor dumb negroes gasping for breath in the foul hold of a transport ship, or driven with whips like cattle to labor in a fetid rice swamp; what we see is human nature, and the "violation of its most sacred rights in the persons of a distant people." The thin vision of things in the abstract rarely reaches the sympathies. Few things are less moving than to gaze upon the concept of miserable death, and it is possible to contemplate "an assemblage of horrors that wants no fact of distinguished die" without much righteous indignation.

Yet the real reason lies deeper. It is of course quite possible to invest a generalized statement with an emotional quality. Consider the famous passage from Lincoln's second Inaugural:

Fondly do we hope — fervently do we pray — that this mighty scourge of war may speedily pass away. Yet, if God wills that it continue until all the wealth piled by the bondman's two hundred and fifty years of unrequited toil shall be sunk, and until every drop of blood drawn with the lash shall be paid by another drawn by the sword, as was said three thousand years ago, so still it must be said, "the judgments of the Lord are true and righteous altogether."

Compare this with Jefferson's

And that this assemblage of horrors might want no fact of distinguished die, he is now exciting these very people to rise in arms against us, and to purchase that liberty of which *he* deprived them, by murdering the people upon whom *he* also obtruded them; thus paying off former crimes committed against the *liberties* of one people, with crimes which he urges them to commit against the *lives* of another.

Making every allowance for difference in subject and in occasion, these passages differ as light differs from darkness. There is a quality of deep feeling about the first, an indefinable something which is profoundly moving; and this something, which informs and enriches much of Lincoln's writing, is rarely, almost never present in the writing of Jefferson.

This something, which Jefferson lacked but which Lincoln possessed in full measure, may perhaps for want of a better term be called a profoundly emotional apprehension of experience. [One might say that Jefferson felt with the mind, as some people think with the heart.*]* He had enthusiasm, but it was enthusiasm engendered by an irrepressible intellectual curiosity. He was ardent, but his ardors were cool, giving forth light without heat. One never feels with Jefferson, as one does with Washington, that his restraint is the effect of a powerful will persistently holding down a profoundly passionate nature. One has every confidence that Jefferson will never lose control of himself, will never give way to purifying rage, relieving his overwrought feelings by an outburst of divine swearing. All his ideas and sentiments seem of easy birth, flowing felicitously from an alert and expeditious brain rather than slowly and painfully welling up from the obscure depths of his nature. "I looked for gravity," says Maclay, giving his first impressions of Jefferson, "but a laxity of manner seemed shed about him. He spoke almost without ceasing; but even his discourse partook of his personal demeanor. It was loose and rambling; and yet he scattered information wherever he went, and some even brilliant sentiments sparkled from him."

Jefferson's writing is much like that — a ceaseless flow, sparkling, often brilliant, a kind of easy improvisation. There are in his writings few of those ominous overtones charged with emotion, and implying more than is expressed.

Sometimes, indeed, by virtue of a certain facility, a certain complacent optimism, by virtue of saying disputed things in such a pleasant way, his words imply even less than they mean. When, for example, Jefferson says "the tree of liberty must be refreshed from time to time with the blood of patriots and tyrants," so far from making us shudder, he contrives to throw about this unlovely picture a kind of arcadian charm. You will hardly think of Jefferson, with lifted hand and vibrant voice, in the heat of emotion striking off the tremendous sentence, "Give me liberty or give me death!" I can imagine him saying, "Manly spirit bids us choose to die freemen rather than to live slaves." The words would scarcely lift us out of our seats, however we might applaud the orator for his peculiar felicity of expression.

Felicity of expression — certainly Jefferson had that; but one wonders whether he did not perhaps have too much of it. This sustained felicity gives one at times a certain feeling of insecurity, as of resting one's weight on something fragile. Jefferson's placidity, the complacent optimism of his sentiments and ideas, carry him at times perilously near the fatuous. One would like more evidence that the iron had some time or other entered his soul, more evidence of his having profoundly reflected upon the

enigma of existence, of having more deeply felt
its tragic import, of having won his convictions
and his optimisms and his felicities at the ex-
pense of some painful travail of the spirit.
What saved Jefferson from futility was of course
his clear, alert intelligence, his insatiable curiosity, his rarely failing candor, his loyalty to
ideas, his humane sympathies. Yet we feel that
his convictions, his sympathies, his ideas are
essentially of the intellect, somehow curiously
abstracted from reality, a consciously woven
drapery laid over the surface of a nature essentially aristocratic, essentially fastidious, instinctively shrinking from close contact with men
and things as they are.

Not without reason was Jefferson most at
home in Paris. By the qualities of his mind
and temperament he really belonged to the
philosophical school, to the Encyclopaedists,
those generous souls who loved mankind by
virtue of not knowing too much about men,
who worshipped reason with unreasoning faith,
who made a religion of Nature while cultivating a studied aversion for 'enthusiasm,' and
strong religious emotion. Like them, Jefferson, in his earlier years especially, impresses
one as being a radical by profession. We
often feel that he defends certain practices and
ideas, that he denounces certain customs or

institutions, not so much from independent reflection or deep-seated conviction on the particular matter in hand as because in general these are the things that a philosopher and a man of virtue ought naturally to defend or denounce. It belonged to the eighteenth-century philosopher, as a matter of course, to apostrophize Nature, to defend Liberty, to denounce Tyranny, perchance to shed tears at the thought of a virtuous action. It was always in character for him to feel the degradation of Human Nature when confronted with the idea of Negro Slavery.

This academic accent, as of ideas and sentiments belonging to a system, of ideas uncriticized and sentiments no more than conventionally felt, is what gives a labored and perfunctory effect to Jefferson's famous 'philippic against Negro slavery.' Adams described it better than he knew. It is indeed a philippic; it is indeed vehement; but it is not moving. It is such a piece as would be expected of a *'philosopher'* on such an occasion. We remain calm in reading it because Jefferson, one cannot but think, remained calm in writing it. For want of phrases charged with deep feeling, he resorts to italics, vainly endeavoring to stir the reader by capitalizing and underlining the words that need to be stressed — a futile device, which serves only to accentuate the sense of artifice and effort, and, in the case of 'the *Christian* king of Great Britain,' introduces the wholly incongruous note of snarling sarcasm, reminding us for all the world of Shylock's 'these be the *Christian* husbands.' Jefferson apprehended the injustice of slavery; but one is inclined to ask how deeply he felt it.

It may be said that Jefferson touches the emotions as little in other parts of the Declaration as in the philippic on slavery. That is in great measure true; but in the other parts of the Declaration, which have to do for the most part with an exposition of the constitutional rights of the colonies, or with a categorical statement of the king's violations of these rights, the appeal is more properly to the mind than to the heart; and it was in appealing to the reader's mind, of course, that Jefferson was at his best. Taking the Declaration as a whole, this is indeed its conspicuous quality: it states clearly, reasons lucidly, exposes felicitously; its high virtue is in this, that it makes a strong bid for the reader's assent. But it was beyond the power of Jefferson to impregnate the Declaration with qualities that would give to the reader's assent the moving force of profound conviction. With all its precision, its concise rapidity, its clarity, its subtle implications and engaging felicities, one misses a certain unsophisticated directness, a certain sense of impregnable solidity and massive strength, a certain effect of passion restrained and deep convictions held in reserve, which would have given to it that accent of perfect sincerity and that emotional content which belong to the grand manner.

The Declaration has not the grand manner — that passion under control which lifts prose to the level of true poetry. Yet it has, what is the next best thing, a quality which saves it from falling to the prosaic. It has elevation. I have said that Franklin had, equally with Jefferson, clarity, simplicity, precision, felicity. If Franklin had written the Declaration it would have had all of these qualities; but Franklin would have communicated to it something homely and intimate and confidential, some smell of homespun, some air of the tavern or the print shop. Franklin could not, I think, have written this sentence:

When in the course of human events it becomes necessary for one people to dissolve the political bands which have connected them with another, and to assume among the powers of the earth the separate and equal station to which the laws of nature and of nature's god entitle them, a decent respect to the opinions of mankind requires that they should declare the causes which impel them to the separation.

Or this one:

Prudence indeed will dictate that governments long established should not be changed for light and transient causes; and accordingly all experience hath shewn that mankind are more disposed to suffer, while evils are sufferable, than to right themselves by abolishing the forms to which they are accustomed.

Or this:

And for the support of this declaration we mutually pledge to each other our lives, our fortunes, and our sacred honor.

These sentences may not be quite in the grand manner; but they have a high seriousness, a kind of lofty pathos which at least lift the Declaration to the level of a great occasion. These qualities Jefferson was able to communicate to his writing by virtue of possessing a nature exquisitely sensitive, and a mind finely tempered; they illustrate, in its subtler forms, what John Adams called his 'peculiar felicity of expression.'

CHAPTER VI

THE PHILOSOPHY OF THE DECLARATION IN THE NINTEENTH CENTURY

PROFESSOR MOSES COIT TYLER, in his admirable *Literary History of the American Revolution*, takes occasion to remark that "whatever authority the Declaration has acquired in the world has been due to no lack of criticism" — that is to say, of adverse criticism.

From the date of its original publication down to the present moment, it has been attacked again and again, either in anger or in contempt, by friends as well as by enemies of the American Revolution, by liberals in politics as well as by conservatives. It has been censured for its substance, it has been censured for its form; for its misstatements of fact, for its fallacies in reasoning; for its audacious novelties and paradoxes, for its total lack of all novelty, for its repetition of old and threadbare statements, even for its downright plagiarisms; finally, for its grandiose and vaporing style.[1]

[1] Tyler, M. C. *Literary History of the American Revolution*, I, 499.

A document against which so much diverse criticism has been directed at least enjoys the merit of not having been forgotten.

If the Declaration has not been forgotten, if it has been much criticized, much denounced and much applauded, if it has never lacked 'friends' or 'enemies,' no doubt one essential reason is that it was an event, or at least the chief symbol of an event of surpassing historical importance, as well as a literary document which set forth in classic form a particular philosophy of politics. In the Declaration the foundation of the United States is indissolubly associated with a theory of politics, a philosophy of human rights which is valid, if at all, not for Americans only, but for all men. This association gives the Declaration its perennial interest. The verdict of history constrained men to approve of the independence of the United States, or at least to accept it as an accomplished fact; the accomplished fact conferred upon the Declaration a distinction, a fame, which could not be ignored, and gave to its philosophy of human rights the support of a concrete historical example. There they were, and there they remained — stubborn fact married to uncompromising theory; bound for life; jogging along in discord or in harmony as might happen; an inspiration or a scandal to half the world, but in any case impossible to be ignored, with difficulty to be accepted or rejected the one without the other.

During the Revolution, as a matter of course, men were chiefly interested in the fact that the colonists had taken the decisive step of separating from Great Britain; the practical effect of taking this step, at this time, rather than the form, or even the substance, of the Declaration itself, was what chiefly engaged their attention. Warm patriots accepted its political philosophy as a commonplace; and for the most part they found the Declaration admirable, both in form and substance, because they believed that the act which it celebrated would have good practical results. "The Declaration will give a new spring to all our affairs," Samuel Cooper wrote, thus expressing in a phrase the gist of contemporary patriot comment.[1]   Those who were ready for *a* declaration of independence readily accepted *the* Declaration of Independence.   They were not disposed to judge it objectively — or, for that matter, to allow others to do so: "I hope," Mr. Whipple wrote to a friend, "you will take care that the Declaration is properly treated." For men engaged in a life and death struggle, the main point of interest was that the official justification of their endeavor, however for-

[1] For contemporary patriot comment, see Hazelton, *op. cit.*, Ch. 10.

mulated, should be 'properly treated' by being heartily approved.

The enemies of the Revolution, with minds similarly obedient to their interests, found the Declaration bad because they deplored the event which it symbolized. American Loyalist opinion was voiced by Thomas Hutchinson, then an exile in England, in a "Letter to a Noble Lord." Systematic by temperament and habit, Hutchinson quoted and commented upon the Declaration paragraph by paragraph. Of its general philosophy, he said little, thinking it sufficient to point out a certain discrepancy between the theory which proclaimed all men equal and the practice which deprived "more than a hundred thousand Africans of their rights to liberty." Nearly the whole of his pamphlet Hutchinson devoted to refuting the charges against the king. His long experience as administrator, his wide and exact knowledge of British and colonial history, enabled him to subject the statements in the Declaration to a minute and searching analysis, and to prove, past a doubt to those who were already predisposed to agree with him, that the charges against the king were "false and frivolous" — absurd in logic and without foundation in fact.[1]

[1] *Strictures upon the Declaration of the Congress at Philadelphia: In a Letter to a Noble Lord.* London, 1776.

Hutchinson expressed the views not only of American Loyalists but of the majority of Englishmen. It is true, some apologetic voices were raised in England. Governor Johnstone was "far from being pleased with the Americans for their declarations in favor of Independency, but . . . they were driven to the measure by our vigorous persecution of them." According to Charles James Fox, the Americans "had done no more than the English had done against James II." But in general the tone of British comment was hostile and contemptuously sarcastic. "The Declaration of Independence," said a writer in the *Scots Magazine*, "is without doubt of the most extraordinary nature both with regard to sentiment and language; and considering that the motive of it is to assign some justifiable reasons of their separating themselves from Great Britain, unless it had been fraught with more truth and sense, might well have been spared, as it reflects no honour upon either their erudition or their honesty."[1]

The most elaborate, and probably the most effective, contemporary analysis and refutation of the Declaration was prepared by an English barrister, John Lind, in a pamphlet which Professor Tyler says was "evidently written at the instigation of the ministry, and sent abroad

---

[1] For British comment, see Hazelton, *op. cit.*, 232 ff.

under its approval." The author points out
that the Declaration consists of certain "maxims," a certain "theory of government," and
certain "facts submitted to the candid world."
Like Hutchinson, he is chiefly concerned with
the "facts." Each charge against the king is
quoted to be refuted; and the general conclusion
which emerges from this long and minute analysis of the "facts" is that they are not true facts
at all, but "calumnies," statements which allege
as usurpations certain measures of government
under George III in no way different from measures under his predecessors which the Americans
had repeatedly recognized as constitutional.
The "theory of government" and the "maxims,"
Mr. Lind despatches in brief space. "Of the
preamble," he says, "I have taken little or no
notice. The truth is, little or none does it
deserve." Not for their merits, but for the
evil they have done, do the American notions
need to be refuted. For this purpose it is sufficient to say that they "put the axe to the root
of all government," since in every existing or
imaginable government "some one or other of
these rights pretended to be unalienable, is
actually alienated."[1]

In France, we are told, the Declaration was

An Answer to the Declaration of the American Congress. London,
1776. See especially, pp. 117, 119, 120.

officially "well received."[1]   Everything considered, to be received at all was to be well received.   Democratic impudence could not well go farther than to ask the descendant of Louis XIV to approve of a rebellion based upon the theory that "governments derive their just powers from the consent of the governed." If the French government received the Declaration, it did so in spite of its political philosophy, because it could not forego the opportunity to take a hand in disrupting the British empire. The alliance which the French government made with "our dear Americans" to achieve this end was nevertheless something more than a mere diplomatic *entente*.   It was approved with unbounded enthusiasm by the people.   To those who, steeped in the political and social thought of the age, were looking forward to the regenaration of France, America appeared as a striking confirmation of their hopes, possessing all the importance of a concrete illustration of their imagined state of nature.   It is not enough, said Condorcet, that the rights of man "should be written in the books of philosophers and in the hearts of virtuous men; it is necessary that ignorant or weak men should read them in the example of a great people.   America has

---

[1] Silas Deane to John Jay, Dec. 3, 1776; quoted in Hazelton, *op. cit.*, 548.

given us this example. The act which declares
its independence is a simple and sublime exposition of those rights so sacred and so long
forgotten."[1]

In France, therefore, where the American
Revolution was looked upon as a kind of prov-
idential confirmation of ideas long accepted but
hitherto demonstrated only in books, the Declaration was cordially approved. "The sublime manifesto of the United States of America
was very generally applauded," wrote Mirabeau
in 1778.[2] In 1783, Lafayette conspicuously
placed a copy of the Declaration in his house,
leaving beside it a vacant space to be filled, as
we are told, by a declaration of rights for France
when, if ever, France should have one.[3] Whether,
in 1789, Lafayette placed a copy of the Declaration of the Rights of Man and the Citizen
in the vacant space beside the Declaration of
Independence I do not know. He may well
have done so. But it does not appear that the
Declaration of Independence suggested to the

---

[1] *Oeuvres de Condorcet*, VIII, 11.

[2] *Des lettres de cachet et des prisons d'état. Ouvrage posthume, composé
en 1778.* (Hambourg, 1782), I, 284. The "ouvrage posthume" was a
mask to conceal the author.

[3] "As soon as he took a house in 1783, he placed in it the Declaration of Independence with a vacant place, 'waiting,' as he boldly said,
'the declaration of rights of France.'" *Mémoires et correspondance du
général LaFayette*, III, 197. Cf. *Mémoires pour servir à la vie du général
LaFayette et à l'histoire de l'Assemblée constituente*, I, 23.

French the idea of a declaration of rights, or that it served as a model for the Declaration of Rights which they in fact adopted.[1] It was the event itself, the American Revolution, rather than the symbol of the event, which exerted a profound influence upon the course of French history.[2] The reasoned justification of separation from Great Britain was based upon particular acts of the British government which did not directly concern Frenchmen, or upon a political philosophy which was already a commonplace of French thought. In France, therefore, the Declaration was celebrated as a great charter of freedom in the history of a people much admired, a charter all the more significant because it formulated, in terse and admirable phrases, those few political maxims which, as Condorcet said, "seem to be no more than the naïve expression of what common sense

[1] The *idea* of a declaration of rights, rather than the *ideas* contained in it, may have been taken from America. This idea, however, was found applied, not in the Declaration of Independence, but in the "Bills of Rights" in the American state constitutions. This question has been much discussed since 1895 when Jellinek published his *Die Erklärung der Menschen- und Bürgerrechte*. The work has been translated by Professor Max Farrand, *The Declaration of the Rights of Man and of Citizens*. For an able critique of Jellinek, see the article by Boutmy in *Annales des Science Politiques*, XVII. For recent literature see Rees, W. *Die Erklärung der Menschen- und Bürgerrechte von 1789* (Leipzig, 1912), and works cited by Rees in his bibliography.

[2] See Rosenthal, L. *America and France: the Influence of the United States on France in the XVIII Century*. 2nd ed. 1882.

should teach all men."[1] To Condorcet, as to Jefferson, the political philosophy of the Declaration of Independence was just the common sense of the whole matter.

Jefferson and Condorcet, as well as most of their immediate contemporaries, no doubt took it for granted that this philosophy, being but the common sense of the matter, would rapidly win universal approval and become the sure foundation of governments throughout the world. But in fact the United States had scarcely assumed that equal station to which the laws of nature entitled it, before the laws of nature, in the sense in which the Declaration of Independence had announced them, began to lose their high prestige. Throughout the nineteenth century, these "naïve truths" which Condorcet thought "common sense should teach all men," were for the most part taken to be fallacies which common sense would reject. What seems but common sense in one age often seems but nonsense in another. Such for the most part is the fate which has overtaken the sublime truths enshrined in the Declaration of Independence.

This is the more interesting since the main political tendency of the nineteenth century was toward democracy, and political democracy

---

[1] *Oeuvres de Condorcet*, VIII, 18.

could be very conveniently derived from the general philosophy of the Declaration. Yet in very few of the innumerable constitutions of the nineteenth century, in few if any of the constitutions now in force, do we find the natural rights doctrine of the eighteenth century reaffirmed — not even, where we should perhaps most expect it, in the Constitution of the United States or the Constitution of the third French Republic. Modern democracy has accepted one article of the Jeffersonian philosophy — that government rests upon the consent of the governed; and this article, in the form of the right of the majority to rule, it has even erected into an article of faith. For this dogma a theoretical foundation had indeed to be found; but it is significant that the nineteenth century almost ostentatiously refrained from deriving the right of the majority from the natural 'rights philosophy as formulated in the Declaration of Independence and in the Declaration of the Rights of Man.

The simplest, the naïve, way to justify majority rule was of course to fall back upon force — the majority has the power, and therefore the right; we decide matters "by counting heads instead of by breaking them," which seems to mean that it is right for the minority of heads to submit in order to avoid being broken by the majority of hands. This idea may sometimes be seen at work in the minds even of those who professed to defend the doctrines of the Declaration of Independence. In the Virginia constitutional convention of 1829, for example, when those who opposed an extension of the suffrage asked for some reasons for that measure "better than the rights of man as held in the French school," Mr. Campbell, undertaking to derive the right of majorities from "the nature and circumstances of men," found the "natural right" of majorities to reside in this, that the majority has the power "either to compel . . . or to expell the disaffected."[1] This defense of natural rights would probably not have commended itself either to Locke or to Jefferson; but as a rough and ready justification of democracy it has undoubtedly had, in the nineteenth century, a much wider influence than the 'metaphysical subtleties' of the Declaration of Independence.

A more sophisticated justification of majority rule was fashioned by Bentham and his English disciples. Bentham's *Fragment on Government* appeared in 1776,[2] the very year of the Declaration of Independence; but it is significant

---

[1] *Proceedings and Debates in the Virginia State Convention of 1829–1830* (Richmond, 1830), 53, 54, 56, 120.

[2] *A Fragment on Government, by Jeremy Bentham.* Edited with an Introduction by F. C. Montague. Oxford, 1891.

that Bentham's ideas were not much attended to until a generation later when everything reminiscent of Rousseau's *Social Contract* was suspect in England. After 1815, with the revival of the movement for parliamentary reform, there began to be a certain demand for a distinctively British road to democracy. What was wanted was a philosophy that would enable Englishmen to be both radical and respectable, a doctrine within the shelter of which one could advocate universal suffrage and at the same time ridicule Rousseau and renounce the "philosophy of the French school." Bentham supplied this need. Rejecting the eighteenth-century doctrine of natural rights altogether, and taking his chief ideas from Hume and Beccaria, he made utility the test of institutions. The object of society is to achieve the greatest good of all its members; do not ask what rights men have in society, but what benefits they derive from it. In the long run no man can decide for another what is good for that other. Each must decide for himself; and so, if you give each man a voice in deciding what is to be done and how, each man to count for one and none for more than one, the result will be to bring about the greatest good of all, or at least 'the greatest good of the greatest number,' which is perhaps the nearest approximation to the greatest good of all. The high merit of Bentham's theory, in an age that looked back to the Reign of Terror and forward to the socialist menace, was that it had the air of saying: I know that you, the majority of men, have the power, and I offer you everything on condition that you stop waving the red flag and keep the peace. Let us get together; instead of fighting, let us vote; instead of breaking heads, let us count them. The very word 'utilitarianism' had a pacific and practical sound; it enabled men to be democratic without thinking themselves visionary, — above all without being thought by others to be pro-French and revolutionary.

If the classic philosophy of the American Declaration of Independence and the French Declaration of Rights proved unacceptable to the nineteenth century, it was thus not because it could be easily made the basis of democratic government, but because it had been, and could again be, so effectively used as a justification of revolutionary movements. The nineteenth century, while progressively democratic, was on the whole anti-revolutionary. In the United States, from the Revolution to the Civil War, the strongest political prepossession of the mass of men was founded in the desire to preserve the independence they had won, the institutions they had established, the 'more perfect Union' they had created. The European world, for half a century after the French Revolution, lived in perpetual apprehension of a new Reign of Terror, and not the least of its difficulties was that of making terms with political democracy without opening the door to social upheaval and international conflict. The classic political philosophy of the eighteenth century therefore survived, in so far as it did survive, chiefly as an aftermath of the great revolutions. It maintained at best a precarious existence among the obscure and outcast parties that were frankly revolutionary, and flourished unashamed only in the full light of brilliant but brief revolutionary days.

In the western world, it is true, the philosophy of the Declaration won notable triumphs in South America, during the twenty-five years after 1808, when the Spanish and Portuguese colonies were winning their independence.[1] In the United States it has even maintained an august official position to the present day. It may still be seen, in the state constitutions, perfunctorily safeguarding the liberties of mankind. The first state constitutions, which were

[1] Calderon, F. G. *Latin America*, 81 ff. Shepherd, W. R. *Central and South America*, 73, 74. For certain declarations of independence and constitutions, see *British State Papers*, I. 1104, 1108, 1136; V, 645, 646; VIII, 570; IX, 698; X, 701, 1076, 1107; XIII, 725; XIV, 940; XVI, 1049; XVIII, 1065, 1074, 1119.

adopted during the Revolution or shortly afterward, as a matter of course made the current philosophy the foundation of government; and revisions of these constitutions in later years, being mainly confined to those points in respect to which strong popular demand made positive changes necessary, commonly left the preambles intact. The preambles of newer state constitutions seem to be copies or adaptations of preambles in the older ones. Thus the phrase of the Massachusetts constitution of 1780 — "all men are born free and equal, and have certain unalienable rights": or of the New Hampshire constitution of 1784 — "All men are born equally free and independent"; or of the Kentucky constitution of 1792 — "All men, when they form a social compact, are equal in rights": — these phrases, with at most slight verbal changes, reappear in most of the Western state constitutions. Why not use these time-honored phrases, since they were in the great tradition, unless there was some good reason for not doing so? In the South, after the rise of the anti-slavery controversy, there were good reasons for not doing so; but even there it was found simpler on the whole to edit the phrases than to omit them altogether. Thus, in the constitutions of Alabama, Arkansas, Florida, Kentucky (1799), Mississippi, and

Texas (1845), the phrase "All men, when they form a social compact, are equal" was changed to read "All *free*men, when they form a social compact, are equal."[1]   No danger in affirming that all freemen are equal, and have certain inalienable rights — particularly the right of property.[2]

The persistence of the political philosophy of the Declaration in the state constitutions must be mainly attributed to the conventional acceptance of a great tradition; particularly so during the thirty years prior to the Civil War, when political leaders, north and south, were ridiculing as fallacies, as glittering generalities, the very principles which were being proclaimed afresh in nearly every constitution of the time. During these decades, the ideas of the Decla-

---

[1] The above paragraph is based upon an examination of state constitutions prior to 1878 as given in Poore, B. P. *The Federal and State Constitutions*, ed. 1878. Cf. for Arkansas, 103, 121, 134, 155; Alabama, 32; California, 195; Connecticut, 258; Florida, 317, 332, 347; Illinois, 446, 466, 471; Indiana, 500, 512; Iowa, 537, 552; Kansas, 580, 605, 609, 615, 630; Kentucky, 654, 666, 684; Louisiana, 755; Maine, 787; Maryland, 817, 837, 859, 888; Massachusetts, 957; Michigan, 983, 995; Minnesota, 1029; Mississippi, 1054, 1067, 1081; Missouri, 1114, 1135, 1165; Nebraska, 1203, 1214; Nevada, 1247; New Hampshire, 1280; 1294; New Jersey, 1310, 1314; North Carolina, 1409, 1419, 1436, Ohio, 1461, 1465; Oregon, 1492; Pennsylvania, 1541, 1554, 1564, 1570; Rhode Island, 1603; South Carolina, 1646; Tennessee, 1673, 1677, 1695; Texas, 1762, 1767, 1784, 1801, 1824; Vermont, 1859, 1867, 1875; Virginia, 1908, 1913, 1919, 1939, 1953; West Virginia, 1978, 1994; Wisconsin, 2028.

[2] "The right of property is before and higher than any constitutional sanction." Kansas (Lecompton) constitution of 1857. *Ibid.*, 605.

ration survived as a living faith chiefly among those who felt that slavery was an evil requiring immediate and desperate remedies. The old Jeffersonian anti-slavery sentiment had disappeared, or was rapidly disappearing, in the South. Cotton was king, and the cotton planters were determined to maintain their slaves at all hazards. In the North, business interests, deprecating agitation as inimical to prosperity, were all for holding fast to the sacred constitution as a prescriptive safeguard of liberty. Liberty they would defend, to be sure — "Liberty *and Union*, one and inseparable." Against this attitude, the radical abolitionists revolted in passionate disgust. Every honest man, they thought, must know that slavery was a damnable crime against human nature; and yet the United States, proclaiming as its birthright that all men are created equal, not only persisted in the crime, but defended it as a necessary evil or a positive good, thus crowning national dishonor with a mean hypocrisy.

With this crime the abolitionists refused to compromise. Let the Union perish, if it must be so, yes, a thousand times! Honor and righteousness are more precious than law and order. There is a higher allegiance than loyalty to the state. The Constitution, cried Garrison, is a "covenant with death" an "agreement with hell."[1] Neither the Constitution nor the general good is the supreme law of the state, Channing affirmed. "Man has rights by nature. . . . In the order of things they precede society, lie at its foundation, constitute man's capacity for it, and are the great objects of social institutions."[2] "We should be men first and subjects afterward," said Thoreau. "It is not desirable to cultivate respect for law, so much as for the right. . . . How does it become a man to behave toward the American government today? I answer, that he cannot without disgrace be associated with it. I cannot for an instant recognize that political organization as *my* government which is the *slave's* government also."[3] In justification of their revolt against the established régime, the abolitionists naturally turned to the Declaration of Independence. From the positive law, they appealed to a "higher law." They would obey, not the Constitution, but conscience; they would defend, not the legal rights of American citizens, but the sacred and inalienable rights of all men.[4]

[1] "To say that this 'covenant with death' shall not be annulled — that this 'agreement with hell' shall continue to stand — that this 'refuge of lies' shall not be swept away — is to hurl defiance at the eternal throne." *Selections from the* Writings and Speeches of William Lloyd Garrison (Boston, 1852), 118.

[2] Channing, W. E. *Slavery* (ed. 1835), 31.

[3] "Civil Disobedience"; *Writings of Thoreau* (ed. 1906), IV, 358, 360.

[4] Cf. *Declaration of Sentiments of the American Anti-Slavery Society in Philadelphia.* 1833. The abolition argument is carefully analyzed

The abolitionists, like the French republicans and the followers of Mazzini in Europe, were but a revolutionary minority. By the great majority, both north and south, they were despised as fanatics and feared as incendiaries. Conservative men in the North did not defend slavery. They recognized it as in itself an evil, and in increasing numbers wished to restrict the spread of the evil, in the hope that, all in good time, it would disappear of its own accord. This they thought might come to pass if men would be patient and reasonable. But they

in Lewis, C. *The Anti-Slavery Argument as Developed in the Literature 1830–1840* (ms. doctoral thesis in Cornell University library). The principles of the Declaration of Independence were defended by some who were not radical abolitionists. Lincoln defended the Declaration as defining an ideal to be attained "as soon as circumstances should permit." *Works*, I, 232. But he carefully refrained from subscribing to the doctrine that natural rights could be conceived as a 'higher law' which justified violent revolution. Seward, in his famous 11 of March speech affirmed that the "laws must be brought to the standard of the laws of God." "The constitution regulates our stewardship. But there is a higher law than the constitution." *Works of William H. Seward* (Boston, 1884), I, 66, 74. The last phrase aroused furious opposition, especially in the South, and Seward, who did not always carefully consider what he was saying, hastened to explain that the phrase did not mean what it seemed to mean. The speech and the denunciation of it inspired William Hosmer to write a book in defense of the idea of a higher law. *The Higher Law in its Relations to Civil Government.* Auburn, 1852. Francis Weyland, President of Brown University, published in 1835 a widely used college textbook in which he defended the Declaration of Independence and brought much learning to the support of the natural rights philosophy. *The Elements of Moral Science* (ed. 1860), 180, 189, 197, 208, 219. Pro-slavery writers were at much pains, during the decade 1850–1860, to refute Weyland.

thought that the abolitionists, with criminal disregard of consequences, were creating throughout the country an ugly temper which threatened civil strife and a dissolution of the beloved Union. They therefore refused to recognize rights that were not constitutionally defined, and sought for a solution of the slavery question in correct judicial interpretation. If the Declaration of Independence, as was claimed, countenanced the wild talk and treasonable acts of the abolitionists, then its self-evident truths must be the veriest abstractions, totally unapplicable to a practical world. "Is it man as he ought to be," asked Rufus Choate, "or man as he is, that we must live with? . . . Do you assume that all men . . . uniformly obey reason? . . . Where on earth is such a fool's paradise as that to be found?" He urged the Whigs to unite against the new Republican party because it was a 'geographic party' which, if it obtained control of the government, would appear to the South as an alien power, "its mission to inaugurate freedom and put down oligarchy, its constitution the glittering and sounding generalities of the Declaration of Independence."[1] *Glittering generalities!* The very phrase practical men were looking for! Only madmen could suppose that the Union

[1] Letter to E. W. Farley, Aug. 9, 1856; Brown, S. G. *Life of Rufus Choate* (ed. 1881), 325, 326.

and the Constitution and all our hard-won substantial liberties should be abandoned for a metaphysical abstraction.

Southern slave owners were ready to deny the self-evident truths of the Declaration long before Rufus Choate pronounced them glittering generalities; yet they were at first somewhat embarrassed by the fact that the Declaration had been written by the great Jefferson. Loyalty to Jefferson died hard. But perhaps Jefferson did not mean what he said. "Our forefathers," Governor Hammond explained, "when they proclaimed this truth [that all men were created equal] to be self-evident, were not in the best mood to become philosophers, however well calculated to approve themselves the best of patriots. They were much excited, nay, rather angry." They were angry with George III; and what they meant to assert was only that kings and nobles and Englishmen were no better than simple American freemen. If Jefferson meant more than that it must be ascribed to the fact that he was unduly influenced by the French school of thought. "The phrase was simply a finely sounding one, significant of that sentimental French philosophy, then so current, which was destined to bear such sanguinary consequences."[1] A God-

[1] "Morals of Slavery," in *Pro-Slavery Argument*, 250.

fearing people, such as the South had now become, could not be expected to follow even Jefferson in subscribing to ideas that were obviously tainted with French atheism. "All this," the Rev. Frederick Ross asserted, "every word of it, every jot and tittle, is the liberty and equality claimed by infidelity. God has cursed it seven times in France since 1793."[1]

To hint that Jefferson was an atheist who did not mean what he said was nevertheless not an adequate defense of slavery. Practical men in the North could pronounce the words 'glittering generalities' and let it go at that. They did not own slaves; they did not even defend slavery, they only accepted it as an existing evil to be dealt with practically. But Southern slave owners, denounced by the abolitionists as criminals, and conscious of a certain air of condescension with which even sensible men in the North regarded their 'peculiar institution,' could not keep an easy conscience without a profound conviction that slavery was a positive good. Profound convictions were not to be nourished by contemplating the compromises of the Constitution. Slave owners, as well as abolitionists, needed a higher law; but the higher law which they needed could not be found in the Declaration of

---

[1] Ross, F. A. *Slavery Ordained of God* (Philadelphia, 1857), 105.

Independence. They could adequately meet the abolitionists, who affirmed that slavery was a flagrant breach of the "laws of nature and of nature's God," by proving that, on the contrary, slavery was in tune with the cosmic harmonies. They had therefore to work out a social philosophy which would relieve them of all responsibility by reconciling society as it is with society as God in his inscrutable providence had intended it to be.

The key to the new philosophy was found in a re-definition of that ancient and battered but still venerable concept of Nature. Continental writers had already achieved this essential task; and it was Thomas Dew, fresh from German universities, who showed the South that natural law, properly conceived, might still be made the sure foundation of African slavery. Nature, he argued, is clearly the work of God, and man is the product of nature — it is "the nature of man to be almost entirely the creature of circumstances." Now, since God has permitted men to enslave each other in every stage of human history, slavery must be in accord with the nature of man. Admit that slavery is an evil; yet, since the God of nature is perfect, "evil is not the sole object and end of creation," but only incidental to some universal good. "Well, then, might we have concluded, from the fact that slavery was the necessary result of the laws of mind and matter, that it marked some benevolent design, and was intended by our Creator for some useful purpose." And so, sure enough, it turned out, upon an unprejudiced examination of history, that human progress, in every stage of development, had been possible only because superior men gained ·leisure and opportunity by subjugating their inferiors. Thus God and Nature had decreed slavery as the price of civilization.[1]

A general principle such as this, which implied that "the actual is the rational," permitted of extreme conclusions: "Man is born to subjection. . . . The proclivity of the natural man is to domineer or to be subservient": "It is as much in the order of nature that men should enslave each other as that other animals should prey upon each other."[2] Well, what if the slave should cease to be subservient and begin to prey? Would it not be in the order of nature

[1] Dew, T. R. *An Essay on Slavery* (ed. 1849), 7, 24. The essay was first published in 1832 as a review of the debates in the Virginia legislature on the abolition of slavery.

[2] Quoted from Harper's *Memoir on Slavery* (1838) by W. E. Dodd, who gives an admirable résumé of the social philosophy of the Old South in his *Cotton Kingdom*, Ch. 3. The pro-slavery philosophy may be conveniently studied in *Pro-Slavery Argument as Maintained by the Most Distinguished Writers of the Southern States*. Philadelphia, 1853. This is a reprint of writings by Dew, Harper, Simms, and Hammond. Cf. also Cooper, Th. *Lectures on the Elements of Political Economy* (Columbia, S. C., 1826); Fletcher, J. *Studies on Slavery* (Natchez,

that the slave should kill his master and run away? And would not the slave who ran away, and the abolitionist who aided him, both be doing God's will, if God permitted the enterprise to succeed? This was perhaps going too far. It needed to be demonstrated that obedience to the Fugitive Slave Law was more effectively in accord with God's purpose than the inclination of the slave to run away. The general principle had therefore to be so stated that the positive law of any particular state would make an integral part of the universal law of nature.

It was Calhoun who performed this task most successfully. "In order to have a clear and just conception of the nature and object of government," he says in the opening para-

Charleston, New Orleans, and Philadelphia. 5th thousand, 1852); Sawyer, G. S. *Southern Institutes* (Philadelphia, 1859); Fitzhugh, G. *Cannibals All! Or Slaves without Masters* (Richmond, 1857); Seabury, S. *American Slavery Distinguished from the Slavery of English Theorists and Justified by the Law of Nature* (New York, 1861); Smith, A. W. *Lectures on the Philosophy and Practice of Slavery* (Nashville, 1856); Campbell, J. *Negro-Mania: being an Examination of the Falsely Assumed Equality of the Various Races of Men* (Philadelphia, 1851). J. C. Nott published his learned ethnological researches to demonstrate the 'plurality of creations.' Cf. his digression on the negro (*Types of Mankind*, 10th ed. 1871, p. 191.). His ideas on slavery were more fully given in an address printed in De Bow's *Industrial Resources*, II, 308. The laws of nature from the physiological point of view also proved that the negro never had been, and never could be, the equal of the white man. Cf. Dr. Cartwright on "Diseases and Peculiarities of the Negro" in *Ibid.*, 315.

graph of the *Disquisition on Government*,[1] "it is indispensable to understand correctly what that constitution or law of our nature is, in which government originates; or, to express it more fully and accurately, — that law, without which government would not, and with which, it must necessarily exist." This constitution or law of our nature he states as follows: "while man is . . . so formed as to feel what affects others, as well as what affects himself, he is, at the same time, so constituted as to feel more intensely what affects himself directly, than what affects him indirectly through others." His feeling what affects others fits him to live with others, in the social state; but his feeling more intensely what affects himself results in a "tendency to a universal state of conflict, between individual and individual," which, if not restrained by some controlling power, will end "in a state of universal discord and confusion, destructive of the social state and the ends for which it is ordained. This controlling

---

[1] The *Disquisition on Government* was not printed until 1851, when it appeared in the first volume of the *Works of John C. Calhoun*. The same ideas, so far as the Declaration of Independence is concerned, were presented by Calhoun in his speech on the Oregon Bill in the Senate in 1848. *Works*, IV, 507–510. Even at that time these ideas were commonplace in the South. The *Disquisition* is important therefore, not from any influence it may have had in determining the character of the pro-slavery philosophy, but because it is the most coherent and carefully guarded formulation of that philosophy.

power . . . is *government.*"[1]   Thus society is
necessary to satisfy men's needs, and government
is necessary to restrain their wickedness;
and both are "natural" because God has so
constituted man that he cannot live without
them.

As government is essential for the existence
of man in society, liberty is essential for his
progress and perfection.

To perfect society, it is necessary to develop the faculties,
intellectual and moral, with which man is endowed. But
the main spring to their development, and, through this,
to progress, improvement and civilization, with all their
blessings, is the desire of individuals to better their condition. For this purpose, liberty and security are indispensable. Liberty leaves each free to pursue the course
he may deem best to promote his interest and happiness,
as far as it may be compatible with the primary end for
which government is ordained.[2]

How far individuals may be left thus free will
obviously depend upon circumstances — upon
the special circumstances external and internal,
of the particular community.

[1] *Works of John C. Calhoun,* I, 1, 2, 4.
[2] *Ibid.,* 52.

It is a great and dangerous error to suppose that all people are equally entitled to liberty. It is a reward to be earned, not a blessing to be gratuitously lavished on all alike; — a reward reserved for the intelligent, the patriotic, the virtuous and deserving; — and not a boon to be bestowed on a people too ignorant, degraded and vicious, to be capable either of appreciating or enjoying it. . . . An all-wise Providence has reserved it, as the noblest and highest reward for the development of our faculties, moral and intellectual. This dispensation seems to be the result of some fixed law. . . . The progress of a people rising from a lower to a higher point in the scale of liberty, is necessarily slow; — and by attempting to precipitate it, we either retard, or permanently defeat it.[1]

Liberty in this sense, which is (somewhat inconsistently) both the cause and the reward of progress, implies inequality of condition. That there must be, in popular government, "equality of citizens, in the eyes of the law," Calhoun concedes. But to attempt to establish "equality of condition" would be to "destroy both liberty and progress."

In order to understand why this is so, it is necessary to bear in mind, that the main spring to progress is, the

[1] *Ibid.*, 55, 56.

desire of individuals to better their condition. . .,. Now, as individuals differ greatly from each other, in intelligence, sagacity, energy, perseverence, skill, habits of industry and economy, physical power, position and opportunity — the necessary effect of leaving all free to exert themselves to better their conditions, must be a corresponding inequality. . . . The only means by which this result can be prevented are, either to impose such restrictions on the exertions of those who may possess [ability] in a high degree, as will place them on a level with those who do not; or to deprive them of the fruits of their exertions. But to impose such restrictions on them would be destructive of liberty — while to deprive them of the fruits of their exertions, would be to destroy the desire of bettering their condition . . . and effectually arrest the march of progress.[1]

From this point of view, the self-evident truths of the Declaration of Independence were fallacies chiefly because they were derived from a false conception of nature. It might well be that all men are equal in a state of nature, "meaning, by a state of nature, a state of individuality, supposed to have existed prior

[1] *Ibid.*, 56, 57.

to the social and political state, and in which men lived apart and independent of each other." In such a state all men would indeed be free and equal.

But such a state is purely hypothetical. It never did, nor can exist; as it is inconsistent with the preservation and perpetuation of the race. It is, therefore, a great misnomer to call it *the state of nature*. Instead of being the natural state of man, it is, of all conceivable states, the most opposed to his nature — most repugnant to his feelings, and most incompatible with his wants. His natural state is the social and political — the one for which his Creator made him, and the only one in which he can preserve and perfect his race. . . . It follows, that men, instead of being born in it (the so-called state of nature) are born in the social and political state; and of course, instead of being born free and equal, are born subject, not only to parental authority, but to the laws and institutions of the country where born, and under whose protection they draw their first breath.[1]

Thus Calhoun identified natural law with the positive law of particular states, the state of

[1] *Ibid.*, 58.

nature with the state of political society as history actually gave it rather than as it might be rationally conceived and reconstructed. In this scheme the natural state of the African race was obviously the state which the historic process created for it in any moment of historical evolution. It might seem a hard saying to affirm that the natural rights of Southern slaves were defined in the Fugitive Slave law and the statutes of South Carolina; but so it had been decreed by God who created men with varying instincts and capacities, and laid down, in terms of these instincts and capacities, the indefeasible conditions under which men must win or lose a precarious freedom.

Whether the social philosophers of the Old South were much influenced by contemporary political speculation in Europe it is difficult to determine. Thomas Dew studied in German universities,[1] where he must have become familiar with the ideas of the historic rights school. Francis Lieber, a German Liberal who took his degree at Jena, was appointed professor of Political Economy in South Carolina College in 1835. There he remained for twenty years teaching the ideas which he doubtless imbibed in his university days, and which in any case he expounded in his *Political Ethics*, first

[1] Dodd, W. E. *Cotton Kingdom*, 49.

published in 1838.[1] At all events, whether German influence was great or little, the political ideas which in the United States discredited the doctrines of the Declaration of Independence were similar in essentials to those which in Europe had already deprived the Declaration of the Rights of Man of its former high prestige.

In Europe, the revulsion from the ideas of the eighteenth century was the direct result of the French Revolution and the Napoleonic conquests. After twenty-five years of political upheaval it seemed to most men that "social regeneration" had been carried, if not too far, at least far enough. Long before that grey dawn of 1815, it seemed obvious that the Revolution had not ushered in the millennium. It seemed to have ushered in, instead of the millennium, the Guillotine; instead of a just and abiding social order, the Jacobin Terror; instead of the religion of Humanity, the blasphemies of Hébert's Festival of Reason; instead of the fraternal concord of people, devastating war and the subjection of nations to the cynical despotism of a military adventurer. So at least most men thought. "The Revolution"

---

[1] "What is . . . the true state of nature of any being or thing? Doubtless that in which it fulfills most completely that end and object for which it is made. . . . Man was essentially made for progressive civilization, and this, therefore, is *his* natural state." *Political Ethics* (ed. 1885), I, 133.

was a phrase which called up, in the minds of solid, respectable people everywhere, terrifying visions of anarchy and atheism; the good it had done was carefully interred beneath the threshold of consciousness, while its evil deeds were held in pious remembrance. It was taken for granted that Napoleon was (what he called himself) the "child of the Revolution," and that the Revolution was but the inevitable result of the loose and licentious doctrines of "Philosophers," the "atheistical French school of thought," above all of the false and vicious political philosophy of Rousseau's *Social Contract.*

To the generation that did its political thinking against the background of the Reign of Terror and the Napoleonic conquests, it seemed that the revolutionary philosophy had proved disastrous chiefly in two respects. By endowing men with inalienable rights superior to those of positive law, it was a standing invitation to insurrection and a persistent cause of anarchy. But the philosophy of the Declaration of Rights not only preached revolution, it preached the universal revolution. Declaring that the inalienable rights were the same for all men and the only sure foundation of political institutions, it implied that the institutions proper to one people were so to all peoples. The practical outcome could be read in the history of Europe from 1789 to 1815. Not satisfied with destroying the foundations of French society, the National Convention, and after it Napoleon, had justified the conquest of Europe on the ground that it was the high mission of France to impose upon backward neighbors its own superior civilization. Those who had defended Europe in the wars of liberation could not but think that a political philosophy which justified the conquest of one nation by another must be false. And so, as the Revolution had created a deep-seated fear of social anarchy, the Napoleonic wars raised the sentiment of national patriotism to the level of a religious faith. Both in politics and religion, conservatism was in the ascendant, and men were predisposed to welcome theories which made for social stability and permitted each nation to hold fast to its established traditions.

The chief task of conservative thought in Europe was accordingly to discredit Rousseau and the *Social Contract*, just as the task of conservative thought in America was to discredit Jefferson and the Declaration of Independence. Many men refuted Rousseau; but the motives which led men to attempt it, as well as the method by which it was most commonly done, are conveniently revealed in the life and

writings of the Vicomte de Bonald. Like
many another French noble of ancient lineage,
Bonald had read the Philosophers of the eighteenth century, and had taken on, as a kind of
conventional veneer, the current ideas of natural
rights. When the Revolution came he accepted
it as the beginning of better days, and even,
for a time, associated himself with it. But
Bonald was a loyal son of the Church. Unable
to approve the Civil Constitution of the Clergy,
he emigrated in 1791; and watching, during
weary years of exile, the course of events in
France, the Revolution at last seemed to him
the very negation of society and religion. In
1794, at the age of forty, never yet having
written a book, Bonald took up his pen "under
the irresistable impression" that it was his duty
to show how anarchy and atheism were the
inevitable results of the fatal theories of the
Philosophers. His first work appeared in 1796 —
the first of many volumes chiefly designed to
lay a theoretical foundation for political and
ecclesiastical authority.[1]

For Bonald, as for Calhoun, the chief fallacy
of the political philosophy of the eighteenth
century was a false conception of nature. It
is significant that on the title page of his first

[1] Moulinie, H. *De Bonald: la Vie, la Carrière Politique, la Doctrine*
(Paris, 1916), Ch. 1.

book he placed the following passage from the *Social Contract*:

If the legislator, misconceiving his object, establishes a principle other than that which springs from the nature of things, the state will not cease to be disturbed until this principle is destroyed or changed, and until irresistable nature shall have resumed her empire.[1]

This was a profound truth for Bonald as well as for Rousseau. But what is the nature of things?

Since modern philosophy has strangely abused the word nature, it is necessary to determine its true sense. The nature or essence of every being is that which makes it what it is, and without which it would not be that being. . . . God has created these beings with the most perfect natures, and has placed them in certain necessary relations, relations that is to say most appropriate to the *attainment of their ends.*[2]

The error of Rousseau was to confound the "natural" with the "primitive." The true nature of a thing is not found in its origin but in its end: the natural state is therefore

---

[1] *Théorie du Pouvoir* (ed. 1843).   [2] *Ibid.*, I, 44.

a state of development, of accomplishment, of perfection. The instinct of man leads him to form societies; and these societies, since they exist, are "in the nature of man." Like man himself, society has "existence for its object, and it must naturally tend toward its own conservation, toward its own perfection, as man by his nature tends toward existence and happiness." [1]

If, then, society as it has developed and as it exists is the very work of nature, how absurd to say, as Rousseau and the Philosophers said: Go to, we will reconstruct society along rational lines, according to the nature of man. Men might as well try to change their own skins as to try, with conscious deliberation, to reconstruct society. "It is not for man to construct society; it is for society to fashion man." [2] Rousseau did not understand this profound truth; and because he did not understand this, he did not understand the true source of law and social authority. The source of law is no doubt the "general will," as Rousseau maintained; but he misconceived the meaning of the general will, just as he misconceived the meaning of nature. The "general will" is not the mere sum of Individual wills, determined by no matter what hocus pocus of compact or

[1] *Ibid.*, 9.   [2] *Ibid.*, 3.

ballot box. "Every being has a will, if it be intelligent, a tendency, if it be material, to attain its end. . . . Political and natural society has an end, which is the production or the conservation of beings."/ Therefore political society "wills the laws or necessary relations between beings; if it wills them, it produces them, or is itself produced by them, since the general will is necessarily efficacious."[1] This is a way of saying that the general will is the sum of those natural influences which shape the life of a people; and since it is God who creates nature and works through it, the general will is the same as the will of God. Thus Bonald sets up, for the purpose of keeping the individual in his place, a doctrine of the social will which functions without regard to what the individual consciously wills. "Man exists only for society, and society shapes him for its own purposes."[2]

For the purposes of this study, Bonald's premises are more important than his conclusions. His conclusions were too ultra conservative to place him in the main current of nineteenth century thought; but few writers enable one to understand better how the Revolution led men to renounce the eighteenth century conception of natural rights, or to see more clearly how, by a slight twist in the defi-

[1] *Ibid.*, 40-42.   [2] *Ibid.*, 3.

nition of nature, the foundation was laid for anti-revolutionary political philosophies.

This revolution in the inner world of thought, born of the desire to prevent revolution in the outer world of conduct, was far more systematically accomplished in Germany than in France, and is associated, in its origin, with a far greater man than Bonald. It was Savigny above all who taught the nineteenth century how to justify progressive changes in institutions without countenancing violent revolution, and how to think of the differing institutions of many nations as being all in harmony with nature and all equally pleasing in God's sight. Savigny's great work was the *History of the Roman Law in the Middle Ages*, the first volume of which appeared in 1815. But he formulated the central idea of the historic rights school the year before, in a pamphlet in which he opposed the current project for a codification of German law.[1] Savigny maintained that any code at that time would be a bad one, because it would be too much influenced by the "shallow philosophy" of the natural law school, whereas a German code, if there must be one, should be based on a thorough knowledge of the history of German law. Law, said Savigny in effect, is not properly "made" by the legislator, any more than lan-

---

[1] *Von Beruf unserer Zeit für Gesetzgebung und Rechtswissenschaft.*

guage is made by the grammarian. Law, like language, is a natural moral product of a people, no more than the persistent custom of a nation, springing organically from its past and present life. The business of the legislator is therefore not to "make" law, but to discover, through historical research, what it is.

The state itself, according to Savigny, is no more to be created by conscious deliberation than law or language. It also springs organically from the life and history of a people. It originates in "a higher necessity, in a creative power working from within. . . . The generation of the state is thus also an aspect of the generation of law, and it is certainly the highest degree of that generation." Even statute law "lives in the general consciousness of a people"; and thus legislation, in its proper sense, is but giving to positive law "an outwardly recognizable form, by force of which each individual opinion may be set aside."[1] Savigny protested that he was far from wishing to close the door to progress. In the preface to his *System of Modern Roman Law*, written in 1839, he said that "the historical view of legal science is completely mistaken and disfigured when . . . so conceived as if, according to this view, the legal culture developing out of the past were set up as some-

[1] *System des heutigen Römischen Rechts* (ed. 1840), I, 22, 14, 39.

thing supreme." On the contrary, "the essence of that view consists much more in the uniform recognition of the value and the independence of each age, and it merely ascribes the greatest weight to the recognition of the living connection which knits the present and the past."[1]

Savigny was not the most popular writer of the nineteenth century, but the doctrine of historic rights was so exactly suited to the hopes and fears of his generation that it entered, almost without effort, as an underlying preconception, into the thought of the time, very much as the natural rights doctrine of Jefferson and Rousseau had entered into the thought of the eighteenth century. The effectiveness of the historic rights philosophy was indeed precisely in this, that it encountered the natural rights philosophy of the eighteenth century on its own ground, and refuted it from its own premises. Admitting that rights were founded in nature, it identified nature with history, and affirmed that the institutions of any nation were properly but an expression of the life of the people, no more than the crystallization of its tradition, the cumulative deposit of its experience, the résumé of its history. It implied that every people has, therefore, at any given time, the social order which nature has given

[1] *Ibid.,* xiv, xv.

it, the order which is on the whole best suited
to its peculiar genius and circumstance, the order
which is accordingly the embodiment of that
freedom which it has achieved and the starting
point for such further freedom as it may hope
to attain. Welcomed because it opened the
door to progress in terms of nationality while
refusing admission to revolutionary methods,
the new doctrine, or the old doctrine newly
formulated, became the accepted creed of all
those who wished to be classed neither with the
reactionaries nor with the revolutionists, those
liberal-conservatives and conservative-liberals
who realized that they lived in a changing world
but ardently prayed that it might not change
too rapidly.

To prevent the world from changing too
rapidly, nothing is more effective than to look
with admiration on the past; and it was probably the historians who did as much as any
class of men to popularize the historic rights
philosophy. With the rise of patriotic nationalism, men of all countries turned to study anew
the origins and the development of national
institutions. With unrivalled enthusiasm, with
admirable patience and ingenuity, historians
devoted themselves to finding out what had
happened in the past of each nation in order,
as Droysen later explained, to "understand

through investigation." And what historians for the most part understood through investigation was how things had come to be what they were, and why they could not after all have been much different — why the law and government of Germany, for example, could not have been the same, and could not in the nature of the case be made the same, as those of France.

In France liberals and conservatives alike turned to the past in order to learn how the Revolution came, why it succeeded in spite of failure or failed in spite of success, why the existing régime was what it was, why it would last indefinitely or prove only a necessary stage to something better or different. Nearly every history of France written between 1815 and 1848 conveys, explicitly or implicitly, the idea that whatever Frenchmen may think of the situation they are in, history will tell them how they came to be in it. Leber, the editor of one of many collections of chronicles designed to meet the demand for historical works after 1815, expressed a common view in his preface: "One seeks in history all the characteristic traits of a people . . . obeying in its movement the peculiar impulsion given to it by its laws, its beliefs, its morality, its genius, its industry, its habits, and its tastes."[1] In 1836 Sismondi

---

[1] Leber, C. *Collection des meilleurs dissertations . . . à l'histoire de France* (ed. 1838), I, xv.

defined, while he protested against, the underlying preconception which so largely shaped the
historical work of his generation. "We seek
in history," he said, "the rights of the present
generation, and not examples for guiding posterity; we ask of past centuries the measure of
the prerogatives of the throne, or of the liberties
of the people, *as if nothing could exist today
except that which has formerly existed.*[1]

But it was in Germany, where the opposition
to the Revolution was most pronounced, that
political history came most effectively to the
support of the historic rights school of juris-
prudence; and among historians no one professed or preached the historic rights idea more
persistently than the friend and associate of
Savigny, Leopold von Ranke, the patron saint
of nineteenth-century historians. Ranke's first
work appeared in 1824. Fifty-six years later,
at the age of eighty-five, the tireless and insatiable old man sat down to write, in no matter
how many volumes, a *Weltgeschichte*, of which
in fact he lived to finish only six volumes. It
was a brave attempt to complete the edifice
which he had so long labored to erect; for in
truth Ranke's whole life was devoted to the
Weltgeschichte, that is to say the history of the
'progress of mankind.' Yet in Ranke's view

[1] Sismondi, J. C. L. *Histoire des français* (ed. 1836), I, iii–iv.

the progress of mankind was strictly conditioned
by the 'individuality of nations.' He thought
of the different nations as collaborating at a
common task, each one at some period taking
the lead and contributing something distinctive,
something proper to its peculiar genius, to the
common possession. It was his plan to write the
history of each European nation at the time
when it made this distinctive contribution, at
the time when it became, as German history
in the time of Luther became, "at once a universal history." [1]

This was a way of conceiving universal history that the eighteenth century would scarcely
have understood. No man, professing a philosophy, was less of a *Philosophe* than Ranke. He
does not, like Montesquieu, seek for that which
is common to all peoples, but for that which is
distinctive in each people. His interest in universal history never disturbs his faith in the
'individuality of nations'; and hence he does
not identify humanity with the universal man,
with "man in general," but with the particular
nation (or great men speaking for the nation),
at the moment when it most clearly exhibits the
nation's peculiar genius or individuality. When
it does this "it enters into relations so intimate

---

[1] Beginning of Ch. 4, Bk. IX, of the History of Germany in the
Time of the Reformation. *Sämmtliche Werke*, V, 102.

with all the powers of the world that its history, in a certain sense, expands into universal history."[1]   This is almost the precise opposite to what the eighteenth century hoped for: the nation, which the age of enlightenment hoped to see assimilated to mankind, is already, in Ranke's scheme, preparing to swallow the Human Race.

For Ranke, as for the generation after 1815, when, as he says, "historical studies developed essentially in opposition to the ascendancy of the Napoleonic ideas," there is indeed no question of discovering the natural rights common to all men, or of constructing institutions appropriate to all peoples, since the individuality of nations is fixed past all changing.   In each state, he says, "some particular moral or intellectual principle predominates: a principle prescribed by an inherent necessity, expressed in determinate forms, and giving birth to a peculiar condition of society or character of civilization."[2]   The historian will note these distinctive characteristics of the different nations, and record the events in which they find expression; and he will do well to record

[1] Introduction to Bk. V of the History of the Popes.   *Ibid.*, XXXVIII, 1.

[2] Introduction to the History of Germany in the Time of the Reformation. *Ibid.*, I, 1.

them just as they occurred,[1] bad and good
together, since thus it is and not otherwise that
God has made men and nations, through whose
actions he indeed reveals himself. This is after
all the ultimate truth, that history is God's
work, which we must submit to, but which we
may seek to understand in order that we may
submit to it intelligently.[2]

The influence of Ranke, through his books
and through his disciples, was wide and profound; and the philosophy of history and of
rights which he professed and which is implicit
in his books, was that of Savigny, was in the
main that of the generation in which he began
to write, that which Hegel perfected and rare-
fied and formulated for that generation in the

---

[1] This phrase of Ranke's, *er will blos zeigen, wie es eigentlich gewesen*
(Preface to the Histories of the Romance and German Peoples. *Ibid.*,
XXXIII–XXXIV, vii), contains the essence of his philosophy of history;
and it is significant of the influence of his ideas that this simple phrase,
the most famous and the most quoted of all of Ranke's words, should
have become a kind of gospel text for historians in the nineteenth
century.

[2] Ranke's ideas as to the significance of history are frequently suggested briefly in the introductions to the various books of his histories,
particularly the *Reformation*, the *Popes*, and the *History of England*.
They are set forth at greater length in his autobiography and correspondence, *Sämmtliche Werke*, LIII–LIV (*Zur eigenen Lebensgeschichte*);
in the articles he contributed to the short-lived *Historische-politischen
Zeitschrift* with which he was connected, *Sämmtliche Werke*, XLIX–L
(*Deutschland und Frankreich im 19 Jahrhundert*); and in the address
delivered upon his inauguration as Professor of History at Berlin in
1836, *Ibid.*, XXIV, 280.

epigram, *Weltgeschichte ist das Weltgericht.* It
is true that Ranke repudiated Hegelianism. But
it was the Hegelian history rather than the
Hegelian philosophy that Ranke rejected; what
he objected to was not so much that Hegel
derived a false philosophy from history as that
he deduced a fantastic history from philosophy.
The philosophy of both men was in essentials
the same: in the dim background God (or the
Transcendent Idea), moving in mysterious ways,
obliquely revealing the cosmic purpose in man
as he is, and in his history, just as it happened.
For half a century this philosophy was the
chief intellectual weapon for combating the
natural rights doctrine of the eighteenth century,
the chief intellectual bulwark for resisting the
spread of French republicanism and the democratic internationalism of Mazzini. The individual, in the eighteenth century emancipated
from prescriptive law and custom, was once
more confined within the complex framework
of circumstance; liberated by the revolutionary
age from his environment in order to reconstruct it on rational lines, he was again imprisoned in the social process. The existing
social order, the particular nation with its
political organization, its law, its speech and
literature, was thought of as the necessary
product of the social process, as the product of

history; and thought of therefore as the state of nature *par excellence*, as the only valid expression of God's purpose, or as the concrete realization of a mysterious Reason of Nature superior to any mere individual reasoning, a kind of transcendental *Vernunft* enclosing and reconciling within its cloudy recesses the verdicts of innumerable and conflicting *Verstände*.

Natural rights in the eighteenth-century sense, in the sense of the Declaration of Independence, could not be a possession of the individual who was thus securely imprisoned in the social process. Rights he still did possess, rights that were even "natural" and God-given in their way; but they were not something to be fought for and won. Since the rights which God and nature gave him were little more than the privileges, or absence of privileges, which the positive law conferred, it was indeed not always easy to tell the difference between rights and wrongs. Perhaps there was consolation in thinking that one's rights or wrongs, such as they were, were useful to that "society" which "shapes man for its own purposes"; and so long as the individual could be sure the purpose was beneficent, and would benefit some one in the long run, he might be content to sacrifice himself for the ultimate good which God could see even if he himself could not. But if the social process should some time cease to be visualized as the progressive realization of God's purpose, the individual was likely to find his prison rather stuffy, might even find it impossible to associate the idea of rights in any sense with conditions that had every appearance of being ugly and meaningless.

This in some measure came to pass in the latter nineteenth century. Much serious, minutely critical investigation into the origins of institutions seemed to show that all things human might be fully accounted for without recourse to God or the Transcendent Idea. At the same time the fruitful discoveries of natural science, particularly the great discovery of Darwin, were convincing the learned world that the origin, differentiation, and modification of all forms of life on the globe were the result of natural forces in a material sense; and that the operation of these forces might be formulated in terms of abstract laws which would neatly and sufficiently account for the organic world, just as the physical sciences were able to account for the physical world. When so much the greater part of the universe showed itself amenable to the reign of a purely material natural law, it was difficult to suppose that man (a creature in many respects astonishingly like the higher forms of apes) could have been permitted to live under a special dispensation. It was much simpler to assume one origin for all life and one law for all growth; simpler to assume that man was only the most highly organized of the creatures (the missing link would doubtless shortly be found), and to think of his history accordingly, as only a more subtly negotiated struggle for existence and survival.

Meanwhile, this view seemed to find striking confirmation in the world of affairs. "The most indifferent arguments are good when one has a majority of bayonets," Bismarck assured his contemporaries; and contemporaries celebrated his work when he made the German Empire by "iron and blood." Cavour won liberty for Italy, as Mazzini said, "by bowing the knee to force," by calling in the aid of Louis Napoleon, the very man who won fame by placing his heel on liberty in France; and in the New World it was not by the sweet reasonableness of Congressional debate, but by force of arms, that freedom was conferred upon the slave. Confronted with these solid facts, "speeches and resolutions of parliament," rational schemes for reconstructing society, seemed indeed of little avail. Industrial exploitation, Machiavellian politics, war — what were these, what had they ever been, but nature's instruments for enabling those to survive who had the power?

In this view of things, neither God nor the Transcendent Idea seemed any longer a necessary part of the social process. The social process would go on very well by itself. But what its purpose was, or whether it would ever come to any good end, who could say? Herbert Spencer, having replaced God by the Unknowable, could only affirm that the social process was one phase of the evolution of all things "from an indefinite, incoherent homogeneity to a definite, coherent heterogeneity." This might be illuminating, but it was not the same thing as Ranke's idea that ultimate purposes could safely be left to God, or as Hegel's notion that the Transcendent Idea was working steadily toward Freedom. Yet it left the individual more diminished than ever, and more helplessly bound. In a universe in which man seemed only a chance deposit on the surface of the world, and the social process no more than a resolution of blind force, the 'right' and the 'fact' were indeed indistinguishable; in such a universe the rights which nature gave to man were easily thought of as measured by the power he could exert. Aggressive nationalism found this idea convenient for the exploitation of backward races; while militant socialists, proclaiming anew the social revolution, and giving but a passing glance at the old revolutionary doctrine of the Declaration of Independence and the Declaration of the Rights of Man, found their 'higher law' in nature and natural law indeed, but in natural law reconceived in terms of the Marxian doctrine of the class conflict.

To ask whether the natural rights philosophy of the Declaration of Independence is true or false is essentially a meaningless question. When honest men are impelled to withdraw their allegiance to the established law or custom of the community, still more when they are persuaded that such law or custom is too iniquitous to be longer tolerated, they seek for some principle more generally valid, some 'law' of higher authority, than the established law or custom of the community. To this higher law or more generally valid principle they then appeal in justification of actions which the community condemns as immoral or criminal. They formulate the law or principle in such a way that it is, or seems to them to be, rationally defensible. To them it is 'true' because it brings their actions into harmony with a rightly ordered universe, and enables them to think of themselves as having chosen the nobler part, as having withdrawn from a corrupt world in order to serve God or Humanity or a force that makes for the highest good.⤏

In different times this higher law has taken on different forms — the law of God revealed in Scripture, or in the inner light of conscience, or in nature; in nature conceived as subject to rational control, or in nature conceived as blind force subjecting men and things to its compulsion. The natural rights philosophy of the Declaration of Independence was one formulation of this idea of a higher law. It furnished at once a justification and a profound emotional inspiration for the revolutionary movements of the seventeenth and eighteenth centuries. Founded upon a superficial knowledge of history it was, certainly; and upon a naïve faith in the instinctive virtues of human kind. Yet it was a humane and engaging faith. At its best it preached toleration in place of persecution, goodwill in place of hate, peace in place of war. It taught that beneath all local and temporary diversity, beneath the superficial traits and talents that distinguish men and nations, all men are equal in the possession of a common humanity; and to the end that concord might prevail on the earth instead of strife, it invited men to promote in themselves the humanity which bound them to their fellows, and to shape their conduct and their institutions in harmony with it.

This faith could not survive the harsh realities of the modern world. Throughout the nineteenth century the trend of action, and the trend of thought which follows and serves action, gave an appearance of unreality to the favorite ideas of the age of enlightenment. Nationalism and industrialism, easily passing over into an aggressive imperialism, a more trenchant scientific criticism steadily dissolving its own 'universal and eternal laws' into a multiplicity of incomplete and temporary hypotheses — these provided an atmosphere in which faith in Humanity could only gasp for breath. "I have seen Frenchmen, Italians, Russians," said Joseph de Maistre, "but as for Man, I declare I never met him in my life; if he exists, it is without my knowledge."[1] Generally speaking, the nineteenth century doubted the existence of Man. Men it knew, and nations, but not Man. Man in General was not often inquired after. Friends of the Human Race were rarely to be found. Humanity was commonly abandoned to its own devices.

[1] De Maistre, J. "Considérations sur la France"; *Oeuvres* (ed. 1875), I, 68.

INDEX

BIBLIOBAZAAR

The essential book market!

Did you know that you can get any of our titles in our trademark **EasyRead**[TM] print format? **EasyRead**[TM] provides readers with a larger than average typeface, for a reading experience that's easier on the eyes.

Did you know that we have an ever-growing collection of books in many languages?

Order online:
www.bibliobazaar.com

Or to exclusively browse our **EasyRead**[TM] collection:
www.bibliogrande.com

At BiblioBazaar, we aim to make knowledge more accessible by making thousands of titles available to you – quickly and affordably.

Contact us:
BiblioBazaar
PO Box 21206
Charleston, SC 29413

LaVergne, TN USA
12 April 2010
179024LV00001B/88/A